Shakespeare's Progress

FRANK O'CONNOR

SHAKESPEARE'S PROGRESS

COLLIER BOOKS
NEW YORK, N.Y.

This Collier Books edition is published by arrangement

with The World Publishing Company.
Collier Books is a division of The Crowell-Collier
Publishing Company.

First Collier Books Edition 1961

Under the title *The Road to Stratford* this book was published in somewhat different form in Great Britain in 1948.

Printed in the United States of America.

Contents

Introductory Note

IN THE WRITING of this essay I have been indebted mainly to Sir Edmund Chambers' *Wililiam Shakespeare,* and *Elizabethan Stage,* as well as to the textual criticism of Professor J. D. Wilson in the New Cambridge Shakespeare. In a more general and perhaps more personal way I am indebted to Dr. G. B. Harrison's popular works, *Shakespeare at Work, Elizabethan Plays and Players,* and *Elizabethan and Jacobean Journals.*

I have been compelled to test for myself the correctness of certain ascriptions to Shakespeare and the possibility that certain works not ascribed to him may really be his. These are things which no literary critic, however unscholarly by nature, can take at second-hand. It would be the negation of criticism to treat *Julius Caesar* as a play of Shakespeare's if there were the slightest possibility that it really was by Marlowe, and to treat *Edward III* as a play of Marlowe's if, as I am now convinced, it is an early play of Shakespeare's. But the fact that I have been compelled to do this and sometimes to disagree with the authorities does not mean that I regard myself in any way as an authority, and where I have permitted myself to doubt, it has been in the spirit of a true child of the Church who unreservedly submits himself to the censure of his superiors.

Preface

THIS LITTLE BOOK is the result of a few years spent in the theater and of the discoveries I made there. The most important of these was that most of the old plays I loved—Shakespeare's, Chekhov's, Goldsmith's, Sheridan's, and some of Ibsen's—could not be satisfactorily produced at all. Another was that a great many modern plays I heartily detested could be produced very successfully and could entertain even myself. The reason, as I soon discovered, was that the former did not create any link between the authors and the actors or between the actors and the audience, while the latter were written by men who were themselves contemporary with the actors and the audience so that the whole action became a communal entertainment. Once, when a dramatization of a little story of my own was being performed, I wrote in a single line of dialogue about Irish which I put into the mouth of a middle-class wife. It wasn't a very witty line; it merely ran "I never did like that language" but, on the first night, when I heard the roar of laughter that shook the theater, I realized to my shame that I could now do what none of my gods and heroes could do, and use my players to communicate directly with my audience. No actor can rouse a laugh with Shakespeare's dirty jokes: they are unintelligible to the audience, usually unintelligible to the actor, and sometimes unintelligible to scholars as well.

I once heard a Shakespearean scholar lecture on Shakespeare's handwriting in the riot scene of *Sir Thomas More* and end by adapting a speech of Malvolio's "Here be his 'C's,' his 'U's,' and his 'T's' and here makes he his great 'P's.' "

I described my disillusionment in three lectures published under the title of "The Art of the Theatre" and see no reason to revise my conclusions. It is clear that Shakespeare's plays moved many of his contemporaries profoundly. All I can say is that they do not move me. What has happened is that the collaboration between author, players, and audience that produces great theater has ceased to exist. Sometimes the dissolution of that collaboration occurs with such extraordinary rapidity that people begin to doubt if the critics of any period are ever in their right minds. It happened after the death of Synge, when *The Playboy of the Western World* suddenly ceased to madden Irish audiences and charmed them instead. This does not mean that the Synge-haters who hissed the original *Playboy,* produced under Synge's eye, were intelligent. They weren't; but neither were they hissing the play that I saw fifteen years later. The same sort of thing happened in France at the end of World War II when Giraudoux and Jouvet were both dead, and people wondered if their memories of the Giraudoux plays were merely youthful illusions. They weren't. The masterpieces we saw were real enough, but those who see them nowadays and for the future will not see the plays that Giraudoux wrote, that Jouvet produced, and that we listened to in enchantment. How on earth can one explain to those who have not experienced it that elaborate underplaying of long, impassioned scenes and the sudden explosive overplaying of an apparently unimportant line that any actor in his senses would have thrown away?

It is the same fate that must overtake any art which depends on collaboration as much as the theater does. What we see, what we hear in a Shakespearean play today is no longer creation; it is criticism, or rather theatrical scholarship. No Elizabethan audience viewing *Hamlet* would have seen in Polonius the tendentious old bore that we see. It would have seen a caricature of some eminent politician well known to the worldly members of the audience. We know, in fact, that it must have seen such a caricature, for in the two earlier versions of *Hamlet,* the German text and the First Quarto, Polonius was called "Corambis" and for some reason of policy this had to be changed. Obviously it provided a key to the identity of the original. Today it is no key, and even if we did know whom Shakespeare was supposed to be caricaturing, it would still not be a key, for it would provide us with no hint as to how the part should be played. I have suggested that the Fortinbras episodes may be linked with a propaganda campaign to secure the uncontested accession of James VI of Scotland—a suggestion that seemed fanciful even to me when I made it, but does not seem so fanciful now that we know more of Elizabethan propaganda. *Richard II* had been used by the Essex faction in precisely this way, and Elizabeth understood its significance. "I am Richard II, know ye not that?" It was an age without newspapers, and great public issues were discussed in general terms, by analogy with the behavior of famous historical figures, in the works of tendentious historians and historical dramatists. Who "Corambis" was, and whom the audience understood under the forms of Fortinbras and

Richard II, are questions unimportant in themselves but very important as part of the atmosphere in which Shakespeare and his fellows wrote and performed. It was an atmosphere of excitement and danger, not unlike that of a newspaper office under a dictatorship in which editor and staff may yet end up before a military tribunal. That is an atmosphere we cannot restore in the theater. Whether Fortinbras is James VI or not, we cannot make a modern audience excited over the question of who is to succeed the dying Hamlet. What was literally a matter of life and death to Shakespeare and his audience is of no concern to us.

As performances of Shakespeare are merely criticism of Shakespeare, criticism is often merely performance. There is Hamlet the philosopher, Hamlet the mother's boy, Hamlet "the man who could not make up his mind." Any standard work on Shakespeare will fill in the fable of the cheerful man who began his dramatic career in the 1590's, became gloomy about the turn of the century, and then after six or seven years brightened up no end and became reconciled to things as they were. As a description of Shakespeare's progress from *1 Henry VI* to *The Two Noble Kinsmen* this is far too vague, and in its implications it is highly misleading.

There is a school of criticism in the United States which holds that there are a hundred great books, and that these books may be read and grasped with no particular recourse to "secondary" criticism: the details of when an author lived, when he died, what his marriage was like, whether he was rich or poor, Conservative or Liberal—indeed, what else he wrote besides his "masterpiece." This I call the "absolute" school, and it seems to me completely unhistorical. "But after all, we have *Hamlet,*" it says complacently. If it *has Hamlet* it does remarkably little to make it more intelligible to us.

My own position is simple. It is that no literary work is an absolute. The writer's medium is much more imperfect than that of the painter or sculptor. Within a short time literature becomes an aspect of history and after a few hundred years begins to become unintelligible, as Chaucer, to all intents and purposes, has become unintelligible, and Shakespeare is fast becoming unintelligible to any but students. The reader who wishes to get the full enjoyment out of Shakespeare must saturate himself to the point of identification with Shakespeare, the butcher's apprentice from Stratford who, having got into trouble with a local bigwig, made for London and became a vagabond player of ill-written plays; who learned late in life that he could write the plays much better than anyone else, and, having acquired a little fortune, returned to his birthplace to play the gentleman amongst those who had looked down on him.

Apart from the plays, we know little or nothing about his life, but the plays themselves form a pattern of a man's existence in this world. Apart altogether from the hints we get in the sonnets and in *The Merry Wives of Windsor,* where he apparently avenged himself on Sir Thomas Lucy for some early grievance, we can see that Shakespeare was an abnormally sensitive man, a man on whom every experience left its mark, and though we usually have no idea what the experience was, we can always observe its traces, as in the obsession with suicide that begins in *Hamlet* and continues to the end of his career as a dramatist. What made him so preoccupied for the last ten years of his literary life with

Those that with cords, knives, drams, precipitance,
Weary of this world's light, have to themselves
Been death's most horrid agents?

Did someone he loved commit suicide, and did he himself actually witness the "maimèd rites" he so unconvincingly attaches to Ophelia whose death was the merest accident? We have no idea of the nature of the wound. All we can say is that the wound is there.

The work of every great writer is to a certain extent an allegory of his passage through life, but this is far truer of Shakespeare than of most other writers; first, as I have said, because he was an abnormally sensitive man, but also because he was, more than most writers, intuitive in his approach to literature, not governed as were, for instance, Ben Jonson, Henry James, or James Joyce, by the theoretical approach. He adopted a manner or a method with great facility and dropped it without fuss when it had ceased to serve its purpose. This became a real weakness in his later years when he lightly took up subjects that he was incapable of handling, but whether as strength or weakness, it kept his work unmistakably his own and unmistakably personal in tone.

Accordingly, the student of Shakespeare should satisfy himself that not only has he the pieces of the pattern in the right order, but that he has all the pieces that are available. He should not take my word for it that *Edward III*, certain scenes in *Sir Thomas More*, and a great deal of *The Two Noble Kinsmen* are

Shakespeare's work, but neither should he take the word of a far greater number of writers that they are the work of somebody else. Above all, he should decide for himself whether what Shakespeare revealed of his own inner life can really be simplified into a pattern of optimism, pessimism, and resignation.

A final word. Nobody who reads Shakespeare should forget that Shakespeare was not only a dramatist; he was a poet as well, and, though it is not as easy to summarize one's impression of language as it is one's impressions of dramatic incidents, it is equally expressive and equally revealing. Shakespeare's language changed almost from play to play, and when, as he sometimes did, he wrote in a few lines after an interval of years, the change in style is so strident that it stops us dead. Beginning as a rhetoric in which the meaning scarcely matters, Shakespeare's language developed through the most elaborate exploration of meaning into a style where once more the meaning seems to lose itself in its own excess.

That is what I understand by Shakespeare's Progress; it is the story of Everyman, written by the man of all men on whom that story seems to have made the deepest impression.

Chapter I

John Shakespeare's Wild Son

WE IDENTIFY William Shakespeare first in the world of letters by a bad joke. Up to the age of thirty it would have needed a surgical operation to convince him that puns about "deer" and "hart" were not the best jokes and the most touching allusions in the world. The only part of the Shakespeare legend we can confidently pronounce true on the face of it is that which says he had to leave Stratford because of a misunderstanding with Sir Thomas Lucy—"Lousy Lucy" as he called him—about poaching. For years his literary capital—apart from a large collection of proverbs which he trotted out on every possible occasion—was an obviously firsthand acquaintance with deer, dogs, horses, and hawks, and when we read his early plays like *Titus Andronicus* and *Henry VI,* certain words begin to stick in our minds as they stuck in his; words like "paling" and "park," "hart," and "single" and "bay," and we begin to gather the impression of a most enjoyably misspent youth. Even without knowing that he had got a girl older than himself into trouble, we should have to agree that there was probably something to be said in favor of "Lousy Lucy," who has had the misfortune to acquire the most ghastly sort of immortality, all because of John Shakespeare's wild son.

A wild boy he certainly was, in spite of the proverbs, who left home not altogether of his own free will and with a certain resentful air of braggadocio which comes out in his plays, even the earliest.

Such wind as scatters young men through the world
To seek their fortunes farther than at home
Where small experience grows.[1]

"Home-keeping youth have ever homely wits," he was to write later, without remembering the fable of the fox and the grapes, and even when he had returned in middle age, a wealthy, well-traveled man, he could still look out complacently at the home-keeping youths of his own generation and fancy them envying him and regretting their lost opportunities.

What should we speak of
When we are old as you? when we shall hear
The rain and wind beat dark December, how
In this our pinching cave shall we discourse
The freezing hours away?[2]

But home-keeping youth have the initial advantage of a settled home, and the adventurous Shakespeare drifted into acting, which was no career for a fastidious young man. On the whole, it was a bad time for fastidious young men who hadn't an independent income. Most of the literary men of Shakespeare's day, though university trained, were outcasts, almost outlaws, with the half-savage, unsocial mentality of their kind. An actor, more particularly an actor who had no share in the company, was far lower in the social

[1] *T. of Sh.*, I. 2.
[2] *Cym.*, III. 3.

scale even than they. The advantage to be gained by his London season was conditioned by the Plague which might banish him for years to the provinces. Even in London he played in innyards and makeshift theaters, in broad daylight and the open air, the companion of clowns, tumblers, and dancers. His theater, with its stage jutting out into the audience, was part of that betwixt-and-between state of things which we associate with Elizabethan England; its architecture which is half Renaissance, half Gothic, and its prose—something rather isolated by its geographical and religious position from the main current of art and thought. So too the plays in which he acted, written by university men who had come down in the world, were less according to "the law of writ" than "the liberty"; less in the manner of classical models than that of a wild, popular art in which only the ornaments came from classical tradition. The fact that he was dealing with a folk art rather than with an established art form was to be a source of much trouble to Shakespeare as a dramatist.

Even the style of performance must have been markedly different from ours, for the protruding stage makes it so difficult for us to imagine how it appeared to contemporaries that we find even a great scholar like Granville Barker writing of "the semi-circle of the audience" as though the Elizabethan actor acted in one direction only. To Shakespeare the audience must have been a circle, and when Hamlet spoke "To be or not to be" he could not have stood facing one way but must have swept about the stage, hurling one phrase to the left, another to the right, like an orator at an open-air meeting. In the same way, when Polonius and he were together on the stage they could not have kept the alignment which modern actors keep but must have moved about one another like boxers and fencers, so that the audience saw them from every side.

We may, accordingly, if we choose, imagine our young scapegrace riding a cheap nag or stealing a lift on the baggage wagon as the weary procession of mummers passed through the hopfields in summer. Outside some little town they would form up in their ragged finery, and, with trumpets blowing and feathered hats tossing, parade the town in the manner of a modern circus. In the innyard they would fall to the erection of their stage, and the afternoon would see the townspeople paying their pennies as they came in off the street, the more respectable paying an extra penny to mount into the sheltered gallery. A trumpeter would sound a blast, and the young man with the long sensitive face and intense eyes would appear and perform his part in one of those preposterous plays which in later life would make him shriek with laughter. The light would fade, the players would perform their dance, and then the audience would go home, leaving him to the freedom of the public houses. The platform and the finery would be packed up—

And all our beauty and our trim decays
Like courts removing or like ended plays.

Coming on toward morning he would wake and hear the trampling of horses and the voices of early stirring carters in the cobbled yard. "I think this be the most villainous house in all London road for fleas" and even as he recorded the phrase, with a smile of amusement, his heart would turn over with self-pity.

O do thou for my sake with Fortune chide,
The guilty goddess of my harmful deeds
Who did not better for my life provide
Than public means that public manners breeds.

All the tragedy of the fastidious man who has to make his living in the theater is in that last unforgettable line.

Chapter 2

Maturity

BY THE TIME we first hear of him in October, 1592, Shakespeare was twenty-eight: already an elderly man by the standards of his day. Even what we learn of him at that time does not, however, enlighten us much.

It seems that the poet and playwright Robert Greene had died, and a publisher had produced "Greene's Groatsworth of Wit," a pamphlet which contains an attack on some rival playwrights, one of whom appears to be Marlowe and the other Shakespeare. This is the passage that seems to identify Shakespeare:

"Yes, trust them not," the pamphlet says, referring to actors generally, "for there is an upstart Crow, beautified with our feathers, that with his *Tiger's heart wrapped in a Player's hide,* supposes he is as well able to bombast out a blank verse as the best of you: and being an absolute *Johannes factotum,* is in his own conceit the only Shakesscene in a country."[1] The first italicized passage is a parody of Shakespeare's "O Tiger's heart wrapped in a woman's hide" from *3 Henry VI*.

Thomas Nashe, the poet, replied to this in a new edition of his own "Piers Penniless."

> Other news I am advertised of, that a scald, trivial, lying pamphlet called Greene's Groatsworth of Wit is given out to be of my doing. God never have care of my soul, but utterly renounce me if the least word or syllable in it proceeded from my pen, or if I were in any way privy to the writing or printing of it.[2]

Then Henry Chettle, a printer and hack writer, added to the squabble in a book that was registered for publication on December 8.

> About three months since died M. Robert Greene, leaving many papers in sundry booksellers' hands, among others his Groatsworth of Wit, in which a letter written to divers playmakers is offensively by one or two of them taken; and because on the dead they cannot be avenged, they wilfully forge in their conceits a living author: and after tossing it to and fro, no remedy but it must light on me. How I have all the time of my conversing in printing hindered the bitter inveighing against scholars, it hath been very well known; and how in that I dealt, I can sufficiently prove. With neither of them that take offence was I acquainted, and with one of them I care not if I never be: [presumably Marlowe] the other [Shakespeare?], whom at that time I did not so much spare as since I wish I had, for that as I have moderated the heat of living

[1] "Greene's Groatsworth of Wit" (Bodley Head Quartos).

[2] "Piers Penniless' Supplication to the Devil" (Bodley Head Quartos).

writers, and might have used my own discretion (especially in such a case) the author being dead, that I did not, I am as sorry as if the original fault had been my fault, because myself have seen his demeanour no less civil than he excellent in the quality he professes [acting?]: besides, divers of worship have reported his uprightness of dealing which argues his honesty, and his facetious grace in writing, that approves his art. For the first, whose learning I reverence, and at the perusing of Greene's book, struck out what then in conscience I thought he in some displeasure writ; or had it been true, yet to publish it was intolerable; him I would wish to use me no worse than I deserve. I had only in the copy this share; it was ill-written, as sometimes Greene's hand was none of the best, licensed it must be ere it could be printed, which could never be if it might not be read. To be brief I writ it over, and as near as I could followed the copy, only in that letter I put something out, but in the whole book not a word in, for I protest it was all Greene's, not mine, nor Master Nashe's, as some unjustly have affirmed. Neither was he the writer of an epistle to the second part of *Gerileon,* though by the workman's error, T. N. were set to the end; that I confess to be mine, and repent it not.[3]

I have quoted these famliiar passages in full because, in spite of their familiarity, they seem to me to be generally misunderstood—no great wonder, considering Chettle's peculiar syntax. As Shakespeare and Marlowe were apparently both satisfied that "Greene's Groatsworth of Wit" was not Greene's work at all, it is hard luck on his memory that almost every writer on Shakespeare should believe him to be the author.

What I gather from the documents is that, for some

[3] "Kindheart's Dream" (Bodley Head Quartos).

reason which is not apparent to us, "Greene's Groatsworth of Wit" was recognized as a forgery. Thomas Nashe was blamed, and, whether or not he had anything to do with it, he took fright. Shakespeare, accompanied by "divers of worship," called on the printer and discovered that the manuscript was not in the handwriting of Greene but in that of the typesetter, Chettle. Either Shakespeare and his aristocratic friends called on Chettle, or Chettle called on them at the theater and explained how he came to make a fair copy of Greene's manuscript before submitting it to the licensing authority. As the proof of this had been in his own possession, we must assume that he also told them that he had destroyed the original. Asked how it came about that a certain publication called "Gerileon" contained an item signed "T.N." which was not Thomas Nashe's work, he admitted his own authorship and blamed the typesetter for the mistake. Chettle was a poor specimen of a man. When Gabriel Harvey later took Nashe to task for the words he had written of "Greene's Groatsworth of Wit," Chettle furnished Nashe with an extraordinary testimonial that begins: "I hold it no good manners, Mr. Nash, being but an artificer, to give Dr. Harvey the lie, though he have deserved it by publishing in print you have done me wrong, which privately I never found. . . ."[4] Clearly, he was in a panic, and could only apologize abjectly to Shakespeare and acquit Nashe of any share in the slander. He repeated his insults to Marlowe, but by that time Marlowe had few aristocratic friends.

But at least he showed us that by 1592 Shakespeare not only had a group of plays to his credit; he had

[4] Nashe, *Works*, ed. McKerrow.

made some influential friends. Within the following months Shakespeare dedicated "Venus and Adonis," and Nashe "Jack Wilton," to the Earl of Southampton. Another friend was probably Lord Strange, Marlowe's patron, who had abandoned him because of the charge of atheism made against him. A third was probably Sir George Carey.

Shakespeare's earliest works consist of a blood-thirsty tragedy, *Titus Andronicus,* a brilliant comedy, *The Taming of the Shrew,* and a group of four historical plays dealing with Henry VI and Richard III obviously written in sequence. *Titus Andronicus* is usually regarded as not being Shakespeare's at all, but I am afraid it is entirely his, and the verbal parallels show that it is contemporary with the Henry VI group, "Venus and Adonis," and a number of early sonnets.

The Taming of the Shrew is also believed to be only partly Shakespeare's, and most editors limit him to the Introduction and the Petruchio-Katharina episodes. Thus, according to both Fleay and Chambers, III. 2. 129-150 is by a collaborator. When two great scholars select from a scene of over 250 lines twenty-one as being by somebody other than Shakespeare, there should, one feels, be something spectacularly un-Shakespearean about them. But look at these two lines which are among the ones they dismiss.

Which once performed, let all the world say no,
I'll keep my own despite of all the world.[5]

What is there about these that is un-Shakespearean? Aren't they, on the contrary, so typically Shakespear-

[5] *T. of Sh.,* III. 2.

ean that no one in his critical senses could imagine them written by anyone but Shakespeare? As we read them, do our memories not supply echoes from all the early plays and sonnets: "Though I once gone to all the world must die"; "My life, my food, my joy, my All the world"; "I care not, I, knew she and all the world"; "For you in my respect are All the World." The phrase occurs in two other places in the play (II. 1. 284 and IV. 2. 35) and the same authorities assign one to the collaborator, the other to Shakespeare. Bless our poor criticism from underminers and blowers-up! There was no collaborator.

Here, too, as in *Titus* and *1 Henry VI,* Shakespeare also strikes the characteristic pose that the author of "Willobie's Avisa" was later to make such fun of; that of the English Ovid, the man who really knew all about women—the most dangerous of all poses for a man to strike.

> *She's beautiful and therefore to be wooed,*
> *She is a woman, therefore to be won.*

He strikes another Ovidian pose we shall also hear more about; that of opposing experience with women to the academic education of his day.

But to the critic, the most interesting plays of this group are the historical plays, for here, in a rough-and-ready sequence, we can see for ourselves how Shakespeare learned his job as a theater poet. The first part of *Henry VI* is a wretched production by any standard; that goes without saying. But that does not mean that it is either a Shakespearean revision of a play by a syndicate of authors or one that he wrote as a member of such a syndicate. I have no idea how it came about that it seems to be the new play of Henry VI which Henslowe records as having been first produced in the spring of 1592, at a time when (as we know from "Greene's Groatsworth of Wit") the fine third part must already have been in existence, unless Shakespeare had been carrying it round with him for years; but I do not for a moment believe in the "hands" that scholars identify with such care, and even Sir Edmund Chambers fails to convince me that "Had Death been French then Death had died today" or "No more can I be severed from your side than can yourself yourself in twain divide" were not written by Shakespeare. Indeed, as I shall show in discussing the sonnets, the second passage is so obviously Shakepearean that if it was written by another hand we are faced with a problem far more difficult than that of how Shakespeare came to write a rotten play.

The second part of *Henry VI* is better only in the sense that it is more competent, and here, at least, there is no question whatever of Shakespeare's authorship, for in the Jack Cade scenes we can all recognize his characteristic obsession with the idea of public order. This was a theme that haunted him to the day of his death. He had a real obsession with mobs, as though at some time he had himself been caught up in one and found himself unable to escape. He draws them with great vividness and even humor, as in the lines he gives the old lady in *Sir Thomas More,* who wished to hear More speak because he had made "my brother, Arthur Watchins, Sergeant Safe's yeoman," but the fear always breaks through. Nothing in *Julius Caesar* is so vivid as the scene in which the mob tears the poet, Cinna, asunder. By the time he wrote *Troilus and Cressida* and *Hamlet* his fear had become hysterical, and in all the later plays tragedy is emphasized by the insistence on the disappearance of class distinctions: "preordinance and first decree," "the primogenitive and due of birth" are falling into contempt; the peasant is galling the courtier's kibe; reverence—that "angel of the world" which "makes distinction between high and low"—is in bad shape; "the odds is gone," "all mannerly distinguishment left out between the prince and beggar"; and the end of the world is obviously round the next corner.

But for all its weaknesses *2 Henry VI* mounts steadily, and one can almost perceive the moment when Shakespeare felt Eleanor and Gloucester come alive under his hands. Clearly, he liked the play, and about 1600 he toyed with the idea of revising it, and scribbled in some revisions on the margin in his mature style.

> *Be what thou hop'st to be or what thou art*
> *Resign to death.*[6]

He also almost rewrote the final two scenes from the entry of young Clifford to York's quest for Salisbury.

> *That winter lion who in rage forgets*
> *Aged contusions, and all brush of time*
> *And like a gallant in the brow of youth*
> *Repairs him with occasion.*

These passages have a unique interest for they show us exactly how Shakespeare worked, piecemeal rather than wholesale. But for the rest the play has all the

[6] *2 Henry VI,* III. 1.

characteristics of the early Shakespeare: the weakness for proverbs, the fondness for sporting allusions, and a certain ponderous, coarse poetic power that can be felt even in half a dozen lines.

The gaudy, blabbing and remorseful day
Is crept into the bosom of the sea;
And now loud-howling wolves arouse the jades
That drag the tragic, melancholy night;
Who with their drowsy, slow and flagging wings
Clip dead men's graves, and from their misty jaws
Breathe foul, contagious darkness in the air.[7]

That is not what we should nowadays call a typical Shakespearean passage as we should call the preceding ones Shakespearean, but it is characteristic of Shakespeare in what critics call his "Marlovian" phase. I do not think it owes anything to Marlowe, whose influence appears much later in his work. Marlowe was the one and only Playboy of the Western World, and I sometimes fancy John Synge must have had something more than an unconscious recollection of him when he christened his hero Christopher Mahon. When Marlowe went the round of the London pubs, roaring out his really atrocious blasphemies and defending unnatural vice and smoking (before King James made smoking unfashionable), he was not so much expressing views that had been arrived at by any known process of reasoning as giving a lep to the east while bringing down the loy on the ridge of his da's skull and leaving him split to the breeches belt. Marlowe's uproarious poetry, like Christy Mahon's, is full of

[7] *2 Henry VI,* IV. 1.

radiance; Shakespeare's, as one can see even from the few lines I have quoted, has no radiance at all. On the contrary, it is leaden and sinister. What Shakespeare has, and Marlowe has not, is weight. He is all the time trying to make his lines carry more weight, and sometimes he loads them so much that he breaks their backs. Even in the seven lines I have quoted there are fourteen adjectives; one can see him at his favorite trick of loading up a noun with adjectives as in "The gaudy, blabbing and remorseful day," or "Who with their drowsy, slow and flagging wings"; and if I had continued to quote I should have had to produce others like "And lofty, proud, encroaching tyranny," and "Upon these paltry, servile, abject drudges." One can see that he doesn't worry very much about the meaning of the adjectives so long as there are plenty of them.

One can also see him building compounds under the impression that a compound is twice as effective as a simple adjective, as in the "loud-howling wolves"; and a glance through this group of plays reveals dozens of them: "gentle-sleeping," "earnest-gaping," "bitter-searching," "great-commanding," and even "dead-killing." In *Romeo and Juliet,* in the firm conviction that five words say five times as much as one, he writes: "Beguiled, divorcèd, wrongèd, spited, slain." Sometimes, by sheer mass, he actually does achieve an effect of extraordinary solemnity. "The gaudy, blabbing and remorseful day" is a fine line, whatever it means, and Queen Margaret's "I stood upon the hatches in the storm" is a magnificent line.

The opening scenes of *3 Henry VI* show Shakespeare in perfect command of this sort of poetry. They contain far finer lines than anything in the previous two parts, but they are the same sort of lines, and the effect they aim at is largely physical—a blow in the midriff or a knock over the head.

That raught [*reached*] *at mountains with outstretched*
arms
Yet parted but the shadow with his hands.[8]

These eyes that now are dimmed with death's black
veil
Have been as piercing as the midday sun
To search the secret treasons of the world.[9]

Richard III is the masterpiece of this period, and a masterpiece it is, for all its violence, coarseness, and vulgarity. It is the same sort of poetry: "I stood upon the hatches in the storm" or "The gaudy, blabbing and remorseful day" are lines that might have come out of Clarence's dream, with its "To gaze upon the secrets of the deep" or "To find the empty, vast and wandering air," and that particular sort of poetry went on for years in Shakespeare's work, even after he had developed a far subtler technique. Even in *Edward III, King John,* and *The Comedy of Errors* we find lines like "Even in the barren, bleak and fruitless air" or "Of the old, feeble and day-weary sun," "And eyeless terror of all-ending night," "Before the always wind-obeying deep," and "Lord of the wide world and wild watery seas."

It seems to me great poetry. It is certainly poetry that aims at a knockout; that tries to make your hair stand on end. The trouble with it is that it is merely

[8] *3 Henry VI,* I. 4.
[9] *3 Henry VI,* V. 4.

poetry. Shakespeare, like Marlowe, was at this time a poet first and foremost, and to every true poet poetry is an end in itself. The medium is more important than the content; or if you care to put it another way, to the poet plays are merely an occasion for fine verse, and the stronger the situation, the better the verse is likely to be. Thus, every poet in the theater has a tendency to melodrama. It was not only the unsophisticated Tudor audiences who liked tubs of blood. The poets got quite a kick out of them too.

> *As for myself, I walk abroad at night*
> *And kill sick people groaning under walls.*

But drama is of a younger house. Poetry is about oneself and other people in relation to oneself; drama is about other people and only about onself in relation to other people; and it is only occasionally that the subject that makes for poetry also makes for drama. Marlowe's plays tell us more about Marlowe than they do about their characters, as do Yeats's and Shakespeare's Henry VI plays.

In life, Shakespeare must have been an energetic, ambitious, passionate man, for all the people in these plays are of that type; but the spectacle of so many people being energetic, ambitious, and passionate together creates an extraordinarily somber effect, as thugh we were being smothered in an atmosphere of subjectivity; and we find ourselves longing to get out again into the air and light. Have you noticed how all the fine lines in these plays are somber? How there seem to be none that have lightness and grace, and how they seem to attract gloomy imagery like mountains and seas, darkness and storm?

Drama happens only when the poet's hard shell of subjectivity cracks, and when he is half in, half out of his shell, like the girl in Hardy's poem of the "Desecrated Churchyard," who dreaded lest "half of her should rise herself and half some sturdy strumpet." The poet must not interfere with his own creation except in the last resort, when his imagination refuses to follow his characters further or when he finally chooses to identify himself with them in the last gesture of all.

When Shakespeare had completed this group of plays he had come to a dead end, had reached at mountains with outstretched arms and parted but the shadow with his hands. But during those years something happened to crack the shell of subjectivity, for even in *3 Henry VI* he was feeling his way toward another sort of excellence, the excellence of *Edward III* and *Richard II*, which have nothing shadowy about them. Out of the roar of the Henry plays comes just one speech that shows us what the next phase in Shakespeare's development was to be—the speech of the pious king, cobweb-thin but piercingly true.

What time the shepherd blowing of his nails. . . .

And:

His cold, thin drink out of his leathern bottle.[10]

And after the thunder a still, small voice. And it was so.

[10] *3 Henvy VI*, II. 5.

Chapter 3

Disillusionment

WE ARE SOMETIMES inclined to ignore one important fact about Shakespeare's life: like many other provincials, he developed exceedingly late. He was close to thirty when *Richard III* was produced. Within five years he was the greatest of European writers; within ten, perhaps the greatest writer who has ever lived. Throughout the plays after *Richard III*, we see an amazingly swift development that one would suppose possible only in an adolescent, and parallel with this we have a group of sonnets that accompany the development and seem to describe a personal emotional disturbance sufficient to account for it. This alone would be enough to justify any curiosity we might feel about them.

The story, so far as we can gather it from the sonnets, is that Shakespeare became deeply attached to a good-looking young aristocrat who apparently refused to marry the girl his family had chosen for him. At the same time he was himself in love with a black-haired married woman—"of noted misbehaviour with old and young," if we are to believe himself. The woman was attracted to Shakespeare's friend and became his mistress, leaving the poet doubly bereaved. It is ironic that our English Ovid should have fallen into the very trap against which Ovid warns his students of the art of love, for, according to him, to tell a friend of a mistress was to lose both.

Unfortunately, if the sonnets do tell us this, which is far from certain, they tell us very little else. They give us no clue as to who the young man was, unless, as seems most likely, he was the "Mr. W. H." of the dedication. All the identifications of him are mere guesswork; they do not tell us when the episode occurred or where. Except for the Marriage sonnets, which were probably in the form of a booklet, they were written from time to time, sometimes two, sometimes four to a sheet, and by the time they reached the printer the sheets had been shuffled and the continuity destroyed.

They are extraordinary poems by a most extraordinary man. The sonnets to the woman begin with jocose compliments and degenerate into something very like scurrility. The sonnets to the friend begin in adoration, but this is soon almost smothered in reproaches and complaints. They oscillate in the most disturbing way between a sociable jocosity and a shuddering sensibility; a sonnet will begin in the urbane convention of courtly love with a line like "These pretty wrongs that liberty commits," and suddenly burst into "Ay, me, but yet thou might'st my seat forbear," which immediately tears the whole delicate web of convention to shreds and makes it seem vulgar and commonplace.

One word in particular is repeated over and over again until it literally dins itself into the reader's brain —the word "all."

Take all my loves, my love, yea, take them all . . .

Take all my comfort of thy worth and truth . . .

And by a part of all thy glory live . . .

For whether beauty, worth or wealth or wit,
Or any of these all, or all, or more . . .

All frailties that besiege all kinds of blood . . .
To leave for nothing all thy sum of good,
For nothing this wide universe I call
Save thou, my Rose, in it thou art my all . . .

Or gluttoning on all, or all away . . .

Sin of self-love possesseth all mine eye,
And all my soul, and all my every part . . .

And thou, all they, hast all the all of me.

To me, at least, this suggests a lacerated sensibility, a man of great sincerity but of such wild extremes of emotion that he was completely powerless against his own attachments; and the very devil for the bright young things of the sixteenth century who must so often have bidden him "take life easy as the grass grows on the weirs." If this was the best the English Ovid could do in the imitation of ancient Rome, he had a lot to learn.

Apart from certain minor readjustments suggested by the Arden editor and Sir Edmund Chambers, no attempt at rearranging the sonnets has ever proved convincing. A simple test is the sequence of ten sonnets on Immortality, in each of which the concluding couplet consoles the Friend for the ravages of time by promising him an immortality of letters. These, at least, should go together, but Professor Tucker Brooke and Sir Denys Bray agree on their further dispersal. Professor Brooke makes the additional and common mistake of treating the first seventeen sonnets (those addressed to a young man who does not wish to marry) as the beginning of the whole series, which on every ground of technique is impossible. The earliest may be a couple of short sequences: one on a journey, the other—a particularly silly one—about eye and heart at war for the privilege of contemplating the friend's beauty. This bit of nonsense, apparently modeled on Constable, probably dates from the publication of Constable's sonnets in 1592. By this time Shakespeare, as we know from Chettle's references to "divers of worship," had some powerful friends. The Friend and he had met in the spring; this was probably the spring of 1592, for the usual date of 1593 is far too late.

The long sequence apologizing for his silence and referring to some rival poet is maturer in style but still far from faultless. In "Greene's Groatsworth of Wit" there is an imagine of "a player that being out of his part at his first entrance is fain to have the book to speak what he should perform" [1]; and in Gabriel Harvey's description of the grief of Greene's mistress, he describes Greene as one "that a tenth muse honoured more being dead than all nine honoured him alive." [2] It is hard to read these without thinking of Shakespeare's "unperfect actor on the stage who with his fear is put beside his part" and his "tenth muse, ten times more in worth than those old nine which rhymers invocate"; and the fact that both occur in the Apolo-

[1] "Greene's Groatsworth of Wit" (Bodley Head Quartos).

[2] Harvey, *Four Letters* (Bodley Head Quartos).

getic Muse sequence may indicate that it was written soon after September, 1592. The sonnets to the Dark Lady cannot be much later. In Daniel's poem "The Complaint of Rosamund," published also in 1592, there is a line "By the revenues of a wanton bed" which seems to be echoed in Shakespeare's charge that the Dark Lady "robbed other beds revenues of their rents." I doubt if these and the Canker in the Rose sequence which preceded them can be dated later than 1593.

This date is also suggested by the two long poems, "Venus and Adonis" (1593) and "The Rape of Lucrece" (1594). They are of fundamental importance in the study of Shakespeare's development, because like the frosty but beautiful Marriage sonnets they are written with a wealth of craftsmanship that Shakespeare rarely expended on everyday jobs. They are generally treated as academic exercises. For instance, according to Dr. Harrison, Shakespeare, being inspired by Marlowe's "Hero and Leander," wrote "Venus and Adonis" (which might be politely described as a poem about a young man who did not wish to get married), printed it, and then set out to find a patron. He found one in the Earl of Southampton (also a young man who did not wish to get married), and Southampton introduced him into his household, where, following the fashion, he wrote the sonnets advising his patron to get married.

I do not think that Shakespeare was influenced by "Hero and Leander" nor am I altogether satisfied that Southampton is the Friend referred to in the Dark Lady sonnets; but anyhow, the trouble with this explanation is that it involves an obvious coincidence;

and Professor Wilson, with characteristic subtlety, side-steps this by suggesting that Shakespeare arrived on Southampton's doorstep one fine morning with a copy of "Venus and Adonis" *and* the first seventeen sonnets, in which a nobleman Shakespeare had never met was addressed as his "dear love" and advised to obey his guardian and get married. Somehow I don't think it happened just like that.

But there is stranger to follow, for Shakespeare and the Earl, according to the same eminent authorities, became fast friends, and Shakespeare entertained the Earl with another long poem, in which a poor man, Collatine, tells a princely friend, Tarquin, of the charms of his wife, Lucrece, and Tarquin, inflamed by the description, goes off and rapes her. Now, about this time, Shakespeare, a poor man, was the lover of the Dark Lady, and *his* aristocratic friend came on the scene and made her his mistress. Shakespeare had such uncanny luck with his long poems that it is small wonder he gave up writing them.

What I suggest, of course, is that if the poems are academic exercises, they are uncommonly prophetic; if not prophetic, they must be an artistic treatment of the situations described in the sonnets. As I feel sure that this is what they are, I find it hard to believe that Lord Southampton, to whom both are dedicated, was really the Friend of the Dark Lady sonnets. On the other hand, he may well be the hero of the Marriage sonnets. There seems to me to be no good reason for assuming that the sonnets all refer to one young man.

There is what seems to me a distinctly personal note about some of the passages in "The Rape of Lucrece" that refer to Tarquin.

Those that much covet are with gain so fond
For what they have not, that which they possess
They scatter and unloose it . . .

This is repeated a little later when we are told that this "ambitious foul infirmity"—

In having much torments us with defect
Of that we have; so then we do neglect
The thing we have. . . .

That "the thing we have" was himself, slighted by a youthful Tarquin to whom he was deeply attached—as attached as only a poor young man can be to an aristocrat who befriends him—is at least suggested by the way the theme re-emerges in almost identical words over a period of twenty years. It first comes back in *Much Ado About Nothing* (1598) with a new concluding phrase that gives it its characteristic form —"Ne'er loved till lost"; the adolescent dream of "Then they'll be sorry."

That which we have, we prize not to the worth
Whiles we enjoy it, but being lacked and lost,
Why then we rack the value . . .[3]

We get it again in *Measure for Measure* (1604): "For what thou hast not, still thou striv'st to get, and what thou hast forget'st"; *three* times in *All's Well That Ends Well* (which was probably the old play *Love's Labour's Won* that Shakespeare wrote about this particular time) with its "You are loved, sir. They

[3] *M. A. N.*, IV. 1.

that least lend it you shall lack you first"; "She whom I . . . since I have lost have loved," and:

Love that comes too late
Like a remorseful pardon slowly carried
To the great sender turns a sour offence,
Crying 'That's good that's gone.' [4]

We find it twice in *Anthony and Cleopatra* of 1607-8—"the ebbed man, ne'er loved till nothing worth comes deared by being lacked" and "she's good, being gone"; in *Coriolanus* (1609)—"I shall be loved when I am lacked," and it makes its final appearance in what was probably Shakespeare's last play, *The Two Noble Kinsmen* (1613).

For what we lack
We laugh, for what we have are sorry, still
Are children in some kind.[5]

The date is also suggested by "Willobie's Avisa," a skit on "The Rape of Lucrece" published in the same year as that poem, 1594. In this, Henry Willobie of West Knoyle in Wiltshire (a real person as Professor Hotson has shown, and a relative by marriage of Shakespeare's friend, Thomas Russell) [6] is described in a vain courtship of Avisa, wife of the owner of an inn called The George or The George and Dragon, which Dr. Harrison, in his brilliant edition of the poem, identifies with the George at Sherborne in Dorset, then the home of Sir Walter Ralegh. It may be

[4] *A. W. E. W.*, V. 3.
[5] *T. N. K.*, V. 4.
[6] Hotson, *I William Shakespeare.*

significant that in *King John,* probably written in the same year, Shakespeare speaks of—

Saint George who swinged the Dragon and e'er since
Sits on his horse back at mine hostess' door.[7]

Dr. Harrison shows that the poem is almost certainly a reply to an attack on Ralegh, against whom a charge of atheism was investigated by a local commission in the spring of 1594. Sir Ralph Horsey, one of the Commission, is satirized under the name of "Caveileiro," but it is not clear what Willobie had done against Ralegh. He is encouraged in his courtship by his friend, "W.S.," "an old player," "who not long before had tried the courtesy of the like passion and was now newly recovered of the like infection," and that this *is* Shakespeare is shown by a parody of one of his favorite cadences which the satirist puts into his mouth—

She is no saint, she is no nun,
I think in time she may be won.

These verses are so like the Ovidian advice to a lover printed as Shakespeare's in "The Passionate Pilgrim" that they may well be from the same poem. But whether or not they are his, they make it plain that he did pose as the English Ovid, the amorous smart aleck, and left himself wide open to ridicule.

The slight circumstantial evidence that might link "Willobie's Avisa" with the sonnets is that the Friend's name seems to have been "Will," which might equally well stand for Willobie, and that there are a couple of sonnets, definitely not in Shakespeare's manner, which

[7] *King John,* II. 1.

refer to Bath, which is close to West Knoyle. That the Friend of the sonnets got the girl while Henry Willobie is supposed not to have got Avisa would, of course, mean nothing: the skit would otherwise misfire. At the same time one must take count of Sir Edmund Chambers' warning that "the like passion" does not necessarily mean a passion for Avisa; it might equally mean a disappointment with another woman—the Dark Lady, in fact.

The most important evidence of all is that of *Edward III,* a play Tucker Brooke supposes to be by Peele, Robertson to be by Greene, and which some Shakespearean scholars believe contains two acts of Shakespeare. I have no doubt whatever that the play is entirely Shakespeare's. *Edward III* was registered for publication late in 1595 and published early the following year without an author's name, and as it is a regular playhouse text of a play that had had its run, it was presumably produced not later than the end of 1593 or the spring of 1594—that is to say at the time when Shakespeare was putting the finishing touches to "The Rape of Lucrece." It deals with a similar subject in a similar way. King Edward makes love to the Countess of Salisbury, who defends herself more effectually than Lucrece, "whose ransacked treasury hath tasked the vain endeavours of so many pens," as the dramatist reminds us. In poem and play (as well as in the Dark Lady sonnets) the offense is magnified by the offender's rank—

basest theft is that
Which cannot cloak itself in poverty.[8]

[8] *Edward III,* II. 2.

The essence of authority is self-control. Thus Lucrece says:

Hast thou command? By Him that gave it thee
From a pure heart command thy rebel will.

Edward himself says:

Shall the large limit of fair Brittany
By me be overthrown, and shall I not
Master this little mansion of myself?

Lucrece says:

The mightier man, the mightier is the thing
That makes him honoured or begets him hate.

Warwick in *Edward III* says:

The greater man, the greater is the thing
Be't good or bad that he shall undertake.[9]

Shakespeare in the sonnets says:

Lilies that fester smell far worse than weeds.

Warwick in the play says:

Lilies that fester smell far worse than weeds.[10]

Plagiarism? I doubt it.

It is even more curious in a play written at the very

9 *Edward III*, II. 1.
10 *Edward III*, II. 1.

time of the sonnets to find King Edward ordering his secretary Lodowick to write sonnets on his behalf to the Countess and then rejecting the first sonnet on the ground that it is inadequate. This is not only first-rate comedy; it seems startlingly personal, and adds yet another question mark to the sonnets themselves.

These are echoed everywhere through the play. In the beautiful love scenes, Edward, interrupted in his love-making by the appearance of the Black Prince, murmurs (as though he were remembering "Thou art thy mother's glass and she in thee calls back the lovely April of her prime" or Lucretius' "Poor broken glass, I often did behold in thy sweet semblance my old age newborn"):

I see the boy; oh, how his mother's face
Modelled in his, corrects my strayed desire.[11]

There is the echo of another sonnet in the magnificent lines on death.

When to the great Star Chamber o'er our heads
The universal sessions calls to count . . .[12]

Perhaps the most startling is the cry of delight with which the Countess of Salisbury welcomes her brother, with its echo of the loveliest of sonnets—"O summer's day!"—a mere catch in the breath like Laertes' "O Rose of May!" or Charmian's "O Eastern Star!"—and the really remarkable fact that one line is the very proverb that forms the theme of the Dark Lady son-

[11] *Edward III,* II. 2.
[12] *Edward III,* II. 2.

nets—"Too bright a morning breeds a louring day." [13]

In passing, I may note that there are some striking affinities with *Measure for Measure* which I do not understand. One of these I must deal with later, but there are others, like "To be a king is of a younger house than to be married," which immediately recalls the mutilated lines from *Measure for Measure*—"Ignomy in ransom and free pardon are of two (different) houses," and the fine image of coining

He that doth clip or counterfeit your stamp
Shall die, my Lord; and will your sacred self
Commit high treason against the King of Heaven

plainly imitated in *Measure for Measure*—"coin God's image in stamps that are forbid." But there are similar affinities between "The Rape of Lucrece" and *Measure for Measure* and they may merely mean that the play existed in an early form as part of a group of works all associated with the Dark Lady entanglement.

But the evidence that clinches the authorship of *Edward III* is the identity of style with other Shakespearean plays of the same period; an identity beyond any possibility of imitation, even if the author of *Edward III* needed to imitate anyone. Whatever the nature of Shakespeare's emotional experience, it had an immediate and pronounced effect on his work, which became more finicking, more restrained, more intellectual. This is particularly marked in his use of what I may call the "reflexive" conceit. "Thyself thyself misusest," says Queen Elizabeth to Richard III. "Myself myself confound!" retorts Richard. Of course,

[13] *Edward III*, IV. 9.

there is nothing unusual about the conceit itself, which is merely a rhetorical way of saying "You abuse yourself" or "May I destroy myself." But there is always an implication of antithesis. Everyone and everything contains its own opposite by which it is saved or destroyed; and this harmonized with a certain duality in the Elizabethan temperament that enabled it to act and at the same time to watch itself acting, and to see in art and literature patterns by which to measure its own behavior, like Lucrece's seeing, in the picture of the Fall of Troy, herself as Hecuba and Tarquin as Sinon.

Again, the conceit is not peculiar to Shakespeare; Daniel, for instance, also has phrases like "thyself thyself deniest" and "greatness greatness mars." But Shakespeare made more use of it than any other Elizabethan writer I know of; in fact, he used it to the point of fatiguing the reader. Adonis, by refusing to become the lover of Venus, like the hero of the Marriage sonnets turns into "the tomb of his self-love to stop posterity." "So in thyself thyself art made away"; "Narcissus so himself himself forsook." There is no hope for Tarquin "When he himself himself confounds, betrays," and he must "himself himself seek every hour to kill." His crime has made Lucrece "herself herself detest." In *Edward III* the Black Prince must "himself himself redeem," and the Countess of Salisbury is not beautiful "if that herself were by to stain herself" ("Herself poised with herself in either eye" as in *Romeo and Juliet*).

The treatment of the conceit in *Edward III* is very elaborate. Warwick says "Well may I tempt myself to wrong myself," the Countess asks the King to "Entreat thyself to stay awhile with me," and he tells her to "take thyself aside a little way and tell thyself a king doth dote on thee." Here the antithesis is complete, and the character treated both as subject and object. It is not, as I have said, an infallible sign of Shakespearean authorship, but when in a scene in *1 Henry VI*, which Sir Edmund Chambers attributes to his "Hand B" and which he sees "no obvious reason for not assigning to Peele," I find "No more can I be severed from your side than can yourself yourself in twain divide," [14] I require a great deal more evidence to convince me that the lines are not Shakespeare's, and Shakespeare's in a very characteristic way.

The conceit is not confined to individuals. Anything that is capable of being personified may be presented as an antithesis of which the two parts are identical, as in "And Time doth weary Time with her complaining" or "And Tyranny strike terror to thyself"—the latter again from *Edward III*. "Light seeking light doth light of light beguile" from *Love's Labour's Lost* is an elaboration of another line from *Edward III*—"With light to take light from a mortal eye." These lines are merely playful, but there are many passages where it is impossible to regard the reflexive conceit in this way, and we are compelled to recognize it as a rudimentary form of casuistry, a method of breaking down the fundamental meaning of words, "setting the Word itself against the Word" like Richard II in prison. That play gives us a striking example in the scene where York betrays to Bolingbroke the details of his son's conspiracy, and his wife argues that he is not to be trusted since "Love loving not itself none

[14] *1 Henry VI*, IV. 5.

other can." (For the contrary view see the sonnet on self-love: "Love so self-loving were iniquity.") York tells Bolingbroke to say *Pardonne moy* instead of "Pardon" and she retorts that "thou dost teach Pardon pardon to destroy" and "set'st the word itself against the word." In the New Cambridge edition Professor Wilson tells us that the second line is part of the old play that Shakespeare was revising—"Thyself thyself revisest," in fact.

That this is a form of casuistry is indicated by the way the conceit is used again and again in scenes where some character is arguing himself out of an oath. The classical example is in *King John,* where Cardinal Pandulph argues altogether too forcibly in this way. Philip, according to him, "makes faith an enemy to faith," swearing against religion, "by what thou swear'st against the thing thou swear'st," which is "in thyself, rebellion to thyself," and since "fire cools fire" and "falsehood falsehood cures" his only hope of salvation lies in being twice forsworn. In *Edward III* there are no less than three scenes in which the argument hinges on a breach of faith. Warwick decides to break the oath he has sworn to the King for the same reason that the Cardinal suggests to Philip, because it involves a contradiction in terms.

> *Well may I tempt myself to wrong myself*
> *When he has sworn me by the name of God*
> *To break a vow made in the name of God.*[15]

It is all very curious, and very personal, and I should be inclined to think that Shakespeare was tor-

[15] *Edward III,* II. 1.

mented by a conflict in himself between Catholicism and Protestantism if it were not that the casuistry seems to be merely part of a greater upheaval that made him question all values.

A very illuminating example of the contradiction in terms is provided by the early passages on death. Put in the form of the preceding examples, the proposition is something like "Death destroys Death": that is to say all we know of death is the fear of it; every time we fear we die, and when we die the fear dies with us, so death may be said to die as well. The corollary of this is that life is merely a continuation of the fear of death, so that by seeking life we seek many deaths.

In the early plays and sonnets we find the proposition in its simple form. "And Death once dead there's no more dying then" of the sonnets becomes "The worst is Death and Death will have his day" and "Fight and die is Death destroying Death" of *Richard II.* In *Edward III* we get the corollary without the proposition: "Since for to live is but to seek to die and dying but beginning of new life."

It may be that Peele (or Greene, as the guessing goes) inferred the proposition, though I do not remember any example of it in such work of theirs as I have read; in which case we may also assume that one of them took a hand in *Julius Caesar* with its "He who cuts off twenty years of life cuts off so many years of fearing death" and "Cowards die many times before their deaths, the valiant never taste of death but once"; and also lent his assistance in *Measure for Measure,* where we are told that "in this life lie hid moe thousand deaths" and Claudio, like the Black Prince, finds that "To seek to live I find I seek to die and seeking death find life" and the Duke tells us that "That life is better life past fearing death than that which lives to fear."

In *Edward III* the fear of death is itself treated as a contradiction in terms, because it is in fact a source of danger. "If we do fear, with fear we do but aid the thing we fear to seize on us the sooner," so that fear too destroys itself.

The spirit of fear that feareth nought but death
Cowardly works confusion on itself.[16]

Or as the Bishop of Carlisle puts it in *Richard II:*

To fear the foe since fear oppresseth strength
Gives in your weakness strength unto your foe.[17]

We read the same thing in "The Rape of Lucrece" but surely, one need not pursue the argument further. Is it not obvious that the two passages on death which follow, the one from *Edward III* and the other from *Measure for Measure,* were written by the same man?

For from the instant we begin to live
We do pursue and hunt the time to die.
First bud we, then we blow, and after seed,
Then presently we fall; and as a shade
Follows the body so we follow death.[18]

Merely thou art death's fool;
For him thou labour'st by thy flight to shun
And yet run'st towards him still.[19]

16 *Edward III*, IV. 7.
17 *Richard II*, III. 2.
18 *Edward III*, IV. 4.
19 *M. for M.*, III. 1.

That *Edward III* is all Shakespeare's seems to me unquestionable; that it was written shortly after *Richard III* and before *Richard II* and roughly at the same time as "The Rape of Lucrece" is highly probable. Its anti-Scottish sentiments would fully account for its exclusion from the Folio. In 1598 there were protests in Scotland against the fact that "the comedians of London should scorn the king and the people of this land in their play."

If I am wrong in believing that "The Rape of Lucrece" is an artistic treatment of the situation described in the Dark Lady sonnets, then the coincidence that Shakespeare should write such a poem before the situation occurred becomes phenomenal, for in *Edward III* not only does he handle the same situation with obvious biographical detail but actually uses the proverb on which the Dark Lady sonnets are based. "Too bright a morning breeds a louring day." I have no belief in either coincidence, and feel certain that "The Rape of Lucrece" and *Edward III* both spring from the same emotional experience as the sonnets, and accordingly conclude that the experience was over and done with toward the end of 1593; and that it was to this experience that the poetaster of "Willobie's Avisa" was referring when in the summer of 1594 he described the "old player," "W.S.," as "newly recovered" from the infection.

But this was no ordinary emotional experience—if, indeed, Shakespeare ever had an emotional experience that was ordinary. It shattered Shakespeare, and turned him from the aggressive, ambitious poet of the *Henry VI* plays, with his traveling salesman's view of love, into the poet of *Richard II* and *A Midsummer Night's Dream*.

Chapter 4

The Early Plays

THE ANTITHESIS of the reflexive conceit seems to have satisfied some fundamental contradiction in Shakespeare's own nature because all through the sonnets he is doing with the personal situation exactly what he is doing with the words. He is breaking down the terms. I do not mean only those sonnets in which he openly uses the conceit: "Thou of thyself thy sweet self dost deceive" and "That 'gainst thyself thou stick'st not to conspire." I mean principally those in which he identifies the Lady and the Friend with himself and himself with both; the same identification we find in *The Comedy of Errors* and *The Two Gentlemen of Verona*. This identification looks literary; it certainly began by being literary, but somewhere along the line it became true.

He asks the Dark Lady:

Can'st thou, O cruel, say I love thee not
When I against myself with thee partake?

He says more or less the same thing to the Friend.

O how thy worth with manners may I sing
When thou art all the better part of me?
What can mine own praise to mine own self bring
And what is't but mine own when I praise thee?

Within a short time he is suspecting the Friend of infidelity with the Dark Lady and using precisely the same conceit.

When thou shalt be disposed to set me light
And place my merit in the eye of scorn
Upon thy side against myself I'll fight,
And prove thee virtuous though thou art forsworn.

Then the Friend becomes the lover of the Dark Lady and we get it again.

Thy adverse party is thy advocate
And 'gainst myself a lawful plea commence.

At the same time he applies the formula to the woman, and on the ground that the Friend is also himself consoles himself half jocosely, half sentimentally with the idea that since she loves his Friend, "she loves but me alone." To admit any blame, the reflexive conceit must be duplicated and negate itself, making a typical bit of early Shakespearean logic, quite absurd but perfectly lucid.

Then if for my love thou my love receivest,
I cannot blame thee since my love thou usest,
But yet be blamed if thou thyself deceivest
By wilful taste of what thyself refusest.

Whatever this is, it is not all jocosity. It reads more like the description of a profoundly subjective nature which tends to regard other people merely as extensions of itself, and tears itself asunder in the attempt to argue that there are no extensions of human personality, that from the beginning to the end it remains forever alone and aloof. It is the little death we must all face, but fortunately for us, we usually face it when we are still adolescent. It is not often that we find it occurring in a man of thirty.

The work reveals this change in a most startling way. First we see the English Ovid at the beginning of his career, the man who knows all about women.

She's beautiful and therefore to be wooed;
She is a woman, therefore to be won.

A little later we see him again in *Titus Andronicus.*

She is a woman, therefore may be wooed.
She is a woman, therefore may be won.[1]

And again in *Richard III:*

Was ever woman in this humour wooed?
Was ever woman in this humour won? [2]

We see him as others saw him, in "Willobie's Avisa," still clutching his Ovid.

She is no saint, she is no nun;
I think in time she may be won.

And then comes the revelation of the sonnets, the sudden cry of the man in the snare:

[1] *T. A.*, II. 1.
[2] *Richard III*, I. 2.

Gentle thou art, and therefore to be won;
Beauteous thou art, therefore to be assailed;
And when a woman woos what woman's son
Will sourly leave her till she have prevailed?
Ay, me, but yet thou might'st my seat forbear . . .

In that last line, am I wrong in thinking that we can hear, in the words of the lovely Welsh epigram, "the sound of the little heart breaking"?

Take one final example from the noble sonnet on self-love ("the most inhibited sin in the canon") with its profound statement of the narcissism that is at the base of all Elizabethan life and art, and notice how the love to self, to evade the contradiction in itself, diverts itself outward (the opposite of the contradiction in *Richard II*—"Love loving not itself none other can").

But when my glass shows me myself indeed,
Beated and chopped with tanned antiquity,
Mine own self-love quite contrary I read;
Self so self-loving were iniquity.
'Tis thee, myself, that for myself I praise,
Painting my age with beauty of thy days.

Is it not certain that at this point Shakespeare, from mere convention and jocosity, has worked down to a fundamental contradiction in his own personality; an egotism so overweening that it can only transcend itself and become abnegation; a subjectivity so overpowering that it can only break free and objectivize itself; that this is the cracking of the shell, the splitting of the personality by which Richard III becomes Richard II, and Aaron, Shylock; Falstaff the hero and Prince Hal the butt? At this period I feel in Shakespeare a duality that is almost neurotic, as though he might quite easily have walked into a room and found himself sitting there. To me it is as though at last the antithesis has become flesh; *I* does not cease to think and feel with the same blind human passion, but on the very summit of frenzy, *I* suddenly becomes *you* and between them a universe is born.

The change can be seen at once in the half-dozen plays that follow: the three "learned" comedies, *The Comedy of Errors,* written at some time before Christmas, 1594, *The Two Gentlemen of Verona,* and *Love's Labour's Lost,* with their companion histories, *Edward III* (1593-94), *Richard II,* and *King John.* A fourth comedy, *Love's Labour's Won,* referred to in 1598 by Francis Meres, has been lost; it was probably the original version of *All's Well That Ends Well,* and the one surviving scene from the old play shows that it was related thematically to the Marriage sonnets. The prose of this scene on the subject of "Virginity destroys itself" is almost a transcription of the sonnets. I know no way of assigning certain dates to any of these plays or determining in what order they were written. They form one group, all done with great care, and with the spidery, almost old-maidish neatness of the sonnet period; but my impression is that *Richard III, Edward III,* and *Richard II* were written in that order, at a lick, and almost without an interval.

It may be only a fancy that the earliest is *Love's Labour's Lost,* which is the last word in literary artifice. Sir Edmund Chambers dates it 1595; Professor Wilson 1593. The latter is probably right, but the play bears clear evidence of later revision. The most interesting effect of this has been a change in the last act. The Quarto prints at the end of the play the mysterious phrase "The words of Mercury are harsh after the songs of Apollo," to which the Folio adds the still more mysterious "You that way; we this way." Of the former, Professor Wilson can only suggest that it "may conceivably have been a comment on the play by someone to whom he [Shakespeare] had lent it for perusal." But obviously "The words of Mercury are harsh after the songs of Apollo" is the entry line for an ambassador, and it would seem that in the original production the clowns and comedians ended their little masque and sang their two charming songs before the arrival of the ambassador, Mercade. The play then ended with the separation of the pairs of lovers—"You that way; we this way"—but the wistful, inconclusive ending was unpopular, so Shakespeare broke up the masque by the quarreling of the comedians in order to give them a re-entry at the end of the play, which thus closes on a happier note.

Another example is a speech of Costard's at the end of IV. 1—"Armado to th' one side, O a most dainty man." The irrelevance of this has troubled several commentators. Actually, it belongs immediately after the exit of Armado and Moth in III. 1, and has found its way here owing to an amusing mistake of Shakespeare himself. He remembered that the cue contained the word "incony"—"my incony Jew!"—and inserted it after a couplet referring to "most incony vulgar wit." It should precede "Now will I look to his remuneration," but like other misplaced passages in the play it strongly suggests that there was a complete revision, and that the jokes about "remuneration" and "guerdon" were written in for Kempe.

Apparently *Love's Labour's Lost* is immensely topical, and the various allusions have been read as a lighthearted criticism of the academy established in his home by Sir Walter Ralegh under the tutorship of the astronomer, Harriot. Ralegh himself is supposed to be caricatured as Armado, Nashe as Moth, Chapman or Gabriel Harvey as Holofernes. Undoubtedly, the members of this group, Lord Strange and Sir George Carey, were people Shakespeare might be expected to be friendly with, but I am quite certain that neither Ralegh nor Harvey is hinted at in any way: the former because it would not have been safe, the latter because such a vindictive man, who was fully aware of everything that went on in London, would never have written as he did of Shakespeare's work if Shakespeare had caricatured him. *Love Labour's Lost* was produced at court at Christmas, 1597—imagine producing a satire on Ralegh before the Queen!

The only topical reference that has been identified with anything approaching certainty is Holofernes' "Piercing a hogshead!" which is generally accepted as an echo of Nashe's "Piers Penniless" and Harvey's gibe about piercing a hogshead—"She knew what she said that entitled Piers the hogshead of wit: Penniless the tosspot of eloquence: and Nashe the very inventor of asses. She it is that must broach the barrel of thy frishing conceit . . ." [3] Undoubtedly, Shakespeare was interested in this literary free-for-all because there are other echoes of it in his work, but I am not sure that the jokes—if you can call them jokes—about "piercing" and "purse" and "hogshead" would not have been equally topical during the controversy about Martin

[3] Harvey, "Piers' Supererogation."

Marprelate (1588-89), in which a Dissenting pamphleteer attacked the Anglican bishops, particularly with the appearance of "Ha' Ye Any Work for Cooper?" which gave rise to a lot of wisecracks about tubs and hogsheads. The joke about Judas hanging himself on an Elder would certainly refer better in a discussion about the dissenting groups, as might the mysterious joke about Holofernes and the Fathers. There is a clear echo of it in:

the corner-cap of society
The shape of Love's Tyburn that hangs up simplicity.[4]

Here the last word should almost certainly be "impiety," and the reference to the corner-cap of Tyburn must be a contrast to the four-cornered cap of the bishops; or, as Lilly puts it: "There's one with a lame wit which will not wear a four-cornered cap, then let him put on Tyburn which hath but three corners." [5] This probably refers to the execution of John Penry, the supposed Martin Marprelate, on June 2, 1593.

The play deals lightheartedly with a group of young men who forswear love for culture and instantly break their vows, and gives Shakespeare a magnificent opportunity for indulging his passion for casuistry. The keynote is the word "forsworn," which rings out here as it does in *King John;* there are masses of logic-chopping and contradictions in terms, and a remarkable identification of the author and the Dark Lady with Berowne and Rosaline. This is beyond question, for though it might have been a coincidence that Rosa-

[4] *L. L. L.*, IV, 3.

[5] Lilly, "Pap with a Hatchet."

line, like the Dark Lady, should be "a whitely wanton with a velvet brow and two pitch-balls stuck in her face for eyes," and an extreme of coincidence that in the almost contemporary *Romeo and Juliet,* Romeo should be "stabbed with a white wench's black eye" (also belonging to a lady called Rosaline), no comic dramatist in his senses, would, unless he were indulging in a private joke, deliberately destroy his heroine's character as Shakespeare does Rosaline's:

> *Ay, and by Heaven, one that will do the deed*
> *Though Argus were her eunuch and her guard.*[6]

This is very like the writing of a man who knows that the girl and her friends are in the theater and will laugh louder than anyone. Berowne, I have always suspected, is a part that Shakespeare wrote for himself. One might also guess that the Dark Lady's name was some form of Rose.

All the comedies have what seem to be echoes of that entanglement. The identification of the poet with the Friend, which is the theme of the personal sonnets, is repeated in the love scenes of *The Comedy of Errors.*

> *O, how comes it*
> *That thou art then estranged from thyself?*
> *Thyself I call it, being strange to me.*[7]

> *As take me from thyself and not me too.*[8]

[6] *L. L. L.,* III. 1.
[7] *C. of E.,* II. 2.
[8] *C. of E.,* II. 2.

We also get the echo of "When thou art all the better part of me" in:

It is thyself, mine own self's better part.[9]

Apart from a few passages, says one editor, "it [*The Comedy of Errors*] might have been written by anybody," though "anybody" here must, I feel sure, refer to the actor who, according to Dowden, wrote the vision scene in *Cymbeline*. If anybody can produce evidence of his identity he may be certain of a substantial check on account from any theater in the world. *The Comedy of Errors* is a brilliant adaptation; the cutting in of the subplot is done with dazzling skill —the skill of the beginning genius for whom literary creation is not yet the business of doing new things but of doing old ones better than they have ever been done before. The play is full of lovely clean strokes of comedy like "God and the ropemaker bear me witness that I was sent for nothing but a rope"; and from few of Shakespeare's plays do I get the same impression that I can hear the writer's own happy laughter as he wrings another squeeze from the dramatic blue-bag.

What one may say in criticism of it is that, like all classical theater, it is unsuited to the Elizabethan stage and is probably more effective in our day than it was in Shakespeare's. The Elizabethan actors, sealed off by the audience like boxers or fencers, were their own background, properties, and lighting. Since in art every liberty implies a restriction, the poet had to shift his scene and lighting as frequently as a film pro-

[9] *C. of E.*, III. 2.

ducer. The platform stage, like the screen, demanded a certain apparent casualness: it made its effects by a series of brief scenes, all with a slight air of inconsequence, as though they had been written in to fill out the time, and by sharp, poetic contrasts of gravity and farce, night and dawn, woodland and town, succeeding one another without a break. In *Troilus and Cressida* a man walks across the stage exchanging a few gloomy reflections with his brother; in *1 Henry IV* a group of carters we have never seen before and will never see again chatter in an imaginary innyard about the absence of chamber pots. It is a mistake in reading Tudor plays to seek for qualities that are not there; a grievous mistake, for example, to imagine that *Richard II* improves, or ever was intended to improve, upon the haphazard structure of the chronicle. Chronicle is the essence of the matter.

The Two Gentlemen of Verona ought to be a more interesting play than it is, as—quite apart from recollections of the sonnets such as we find in *The Comedy of Errors*—it has a distinctly personal note. It must be almost contemporary with *The Comedy of Errors,* for it is shaped exactly like it, and, though romantic in content, has the same urbane lack of romantic color. It may be based on an older play, but at another remove is certainly based on the story of Felix and Felismena in Montemayor's endless and pointless romance, *Diana in Love.* In that story Felismena (Shakespeare's Julia) is courted by Felix (Proteus) with the help of her maid. Felix leaves and Felismena, disguised as a boy, goes in pursuit. She puts up at an inn in the town where she knows him to be. Late that night she is summoned by the landlord to listen to a serenade that is being given to Lady Celia (Shakespeare's Sylvia) and recognizes the voice of her faithless lover's serving man. Later she becomes Felix' page and courts Celia on his behalf. Like Olivia in *Twelfth Night,* Celia falls in love with Felismena and dies of grief. Felismena takes to the road again, and after many adventures finds a man being attacked by several knights. When she has rescued him she discovers that it is Felix, and he penitently marries her.

The later development of the plot was abandoned by Shakespeare as it did not suit the subplot he tagged on to it. *His* Proteus not only deceives Julia, but also his friend, Valentine, who is Sylvia's sweetheart. If one accepts at all the view that there is a factual element in the sonnets (and I see no way of escaping it), one is bound to admit that the subplot identifies Proteus with the Tarquin of the Dark Lady sonnets—the *third* literary work in which Shakespeare went over the ground—and to spare some sympathy for the unfortunate young nobleman who happened to cross the thin-skinned and exacting poet in his love affair.

In spite of a wretched text, the play moves beautifully up to the last act, and then goes to pieces. The last act is not Shakespeare's, for whoever cut down the play for indoor performance did not think it exciting enough and substituted an ending of his own. Sylvia's father, the Duke, wishes her to marry Thurio, also a duke, and exiles Valentine, who takes refuge with some outlaws in the woods. Sylvia, escorted by the gallant Sir Eglamour, sets out to join him, and is pursued by the faithless Proteus, Julia (still disguised as a page), the Duke, and Thurio. Sylvia and her escort are attacked by the outlaws, and Sir Eglamour mysteriously runs away. She is rescued by Proteus who, finding her at his mercy, decides to rape her, and she is saved only by the appearance of Valentine. Then Proteus repents and Valentine generously says "All that was mine in Sylvia I give thee"; Julia faints—as well she might—her identity is revealed, and everythings ends happily for everybody except the audience, who for two hours have been patiently waiting for somebody to break Proteus' neck.

That the play was cut and the last act botched is shown by Professor Wilson in the New Cambridge edition of the play, and his conclusions are substantially correct. Sir Edmund Chambers does not think that any scenes or incidents have been omitted, but at least one, overlooked even by Professor Wilson, will be obvious to anyone who understands the theater. In the last scene of the so-called second act, we see Julia deciding to dress up as a man and go in search of Proteus. In the second scene of the fourth act (an exceedingly wide gap) we find Proteus, Thurio, and the musicians ready to serenade Sylvia. There enter two figures, a man and a boy, and the following brief dialogue ensues, immediately before "Who is Sylvia?" For the purpose of the illustration I conceal the identity of the pair.

—— Now, my young guest, methinks you're allycholy:
I pray you, why is it?
—— Marry, mine host, because I cannot be merry.
—— Come, we'll have you merry: I'll bring you where you shall hear music, and see the gentleman you asked for.
—— But shall I hear him speak?
—— Ay, that you shall.

—— That will be music.
—— Hark! Hark!
—— Is he among these?
—— Ay; but peace! let's hear 'em.[10]

Now, from this snatch of dialogue, if we accept Sir Edmund Chambers' view, an Elizabethan audience tumbled to the fact that the boy was Julia, whom they had previously seen only as a girl (a much more serious difficulty then than now as the audience had no means of knowing whether a boy represented a real boy or a girl masquerading as a boy); that she was no longer in Verona, where they had last seen her; that she had put up at an inn where she had inquired for Proteus, and that the gentleman escorting her was in fact the landlord of that inn! All that from a casual "my young guest" and an equally casual "mine host." This is the sort of thing that makes a theater man smile; *his* points have to be made so much more brutally. Even with a cast that needed no doubling of parts, and a woman to play the part of Julia, it would still be impossible to convey all the information that the scenario requires in a few lines like these. The source shows what has happened: the scene in the inn has been awkwardly telescoped into the scene under Sylvia's window, and the whole carefully built-up structure of emotion leading to Julia's disillusionment has been demolished.

A glance through *Diana in Love* shows what the original ending must have been. Sylvia and Sir Eglamour must have been taken prisoner by the outlaws in the absence of Valentine. Then the outlaws must

[10] *T. G. V.*, IV. 2.

have attacked Proteus and Julia and been driven off by Julia. Only then would Valentine and Sylvia have appeared, and in explaining his pursuit of her, Proteus would have had to admit his treachery. It may be that at this point Valentine did actually use the line "All that was mine in Sylvia I give thee," which is far too close an echo of "Take all my loves, my love, yea, take them all" to be lightly discarded as an invention of the botcher.

Again, what has happened is that the botcher, having to cut down the play for performance in a private house or an indoor theater, realized that only Sir Eglamour's character stood between him and the possibility of telescoping the two scenes that tied up the two original plots independently, as well as giving the play the added beauty of a projected rape. A man of the theater with a facility for writing verse could undo a lot of the damage, and I suspect that careful restoration would show *The Two Gentlemen* as a play of great charm and a worthy companion piece to *The Comedy of Errors.*

Chapter 5

The Early Tragedies

WHEN HE HAD WRITTEN *Richard III,* Shakespeare had come to the end of the York and Lancaster series so far as he could handle it, and I feel sure that without a break he switched back and began again at the other end with *Edward III* and *Richard II.* As I have said, there is no doubt in my mind that the first two acts of the former play, dealing with the courtship of the Countess of Salisbury, were inspired by the Dark Lady episode and are contemporary with the treatment of the same subject in "The Rape of Lucrece."

But the contrast with *Richard III* is startling. The dramatic method is a rudimentary form of the method that Shakespeare was to stick to off and on for the next ten years. He throws over the playboy type of hero exemplified in *Richard III*. In literature, character cannot be expressed through pure feeling. By its very nature character is ambiguous and can be represented only by the focusing of two independent pictures in one. Usually, one gets this stereoscopic effect when the tragic image blends with the comic one—"Reality is expressed through contradiction," as Yeats used to quote. We can see this very clearly if we compare the wooing of Anne in *Richard III* with the wooing of the Countess of Salisbury in *Edward III*. Anne and Richard are cut from the same piece of material. It is only an accident that Anne is the widow of Richard's victim, and she does no violence to her own nature when she becomes the murderer's wife. The typical Ovidian figure of the early Shakespeare, "she is no saint, she is no nun." But the Countess is a very different sort of person from Edward, and though Edward, like Richard, is willing to wade through rivers of blood to get what he wants, he is also capable of absurdity, tenderness, and even nobility. At the very height of his love-making, the Black Prince enters and makes Edward think of the Black Prince's black mother, so that the dream of passion is dissipated for a moment.

I see the boy, O how his mother's face,
Modelled in his, corrects my strayed desire! [1]

[1] *Edward III*, II. 2.

Even at the most intense part of the action, Shakespeare is not afraid to stand back and poke fun at him, a liberty one could hardly take with Richard. According to Tucker Brooke the play does not contain "a vestige of comedy," but there are few scenes in the early Shakespeare so amusing as that in which the King, having ordered his secretary to write sonnets to the Countess, rejects the first sonnet because it seems to him inadequate. This is not only excellent comedy; it is autobiographical comedy.

Unfortunately, *Edward III* is impossible in a modern theater unless we treat the first two acts as an independent play; for they contain an absolutely magnificent part for a star actress, whose very existence is forgotten after the second act, and scenes equal in power to any in the great tragedies. No modern audience would tolerate such an anticlimax. But Shakespeare was not writing for a modern audience; he was writing for one that paid its pennies to hear all about its ancestors and how they had given hell to the Scots and French.

Indeed, the most Shakespearean scene of all is that before the battle of Poitiers. The Black Prince's speech, as Shakespeare got it from Froissart, was a typical bit of military rhetoric. "Now, my gallant fellows, what though we be but a small body compared to the army of our enemies, do not let us be cast down on that account, for victory does not always follow numbers, but where the Almighty God pleases to bestow it," etc. etc. Audley's speech is the same sort of stuff. "Dear sir, I must now acquaint you that formerly I made a vow, if ever I should be engaged in any battle where the king your father or any of his sons were, that I should be foremost in the attack, and the best combatant on his side or die in the attempt."

Shakespeare's mood at the time can be seen perfectly in his treatment of this material. There was no difficulty in turning Froissart into blank verse; he could do it on his head, and if certain speeches in *Henry V* can be considered a fair example, he frequently did. Instead of doing that he suddenly withdraws himself completely from the action, and, thinking of his beloved contradiction in terms, breaks into pure lyric poetry.

PRINCE: Thou art a married man in this distress
But danger wooes me as a blushing maid:
Teach me an answer to this perilous time.

AUDLEY: To die is all as common as to live:
The one inchwise, the other holds in chase;
For from the instant we begin to live
We do pursue and hunt the time to die:
First bud we, then we blow, and after seed,
Then presently we fall; and as a shade
Follows the body, so we follow death.

This is not the method of *Richard III;* clearly it is the method of *Richard II*. Some supposed borrowings by Daniel between two editions of his great poem, "The Civil Wars," have caused the latter play to be dated 1595, but since Professor Wilson exploded this theory it is hard to see how Shakespeare's play could have been written after Daniel's poem, since historically and critically it immediately follows *Edward III*, probably in the spring of 1594. It is a sequel to an excellent play about Thomas of Woodstock, which is probably the work of Shakespeare's friend, Michael Drayton. The characters are still rather stiff: there is a Welsh captain to whom Holinshed's lines on the withering of the bay trees are given, but nothing else shows him to be a fellow countryman of Glendower; we meet Hotspur for the first time, but, so far as the audience is concerned, his name might as well be Coldspur. Nowhere does the treatment compare with Daniel's masterly narrative. In the poem the popular hero, Bolingbroke, approaches Richard's favorite, Norfolk, with complaints of the government that Bolingbroke hopes Norfolk may help to remedy. Instead, Norfolk repeats the complaints to Richard, who takes them personally and confronts Bolingbroke with them. Bolingbroke returns the accusations of disloyalty on Norfolk, and the stage is set for their single combat at Coventry when Richard, realizing that a victory for Bolingbroke will only increase his already dangerous popularity, resolves the problem by exiling enemy and friend alike. Instead of this admirable intrigue, Shakespeare has only the empty pageantry of Holinshed.

But halfway through the play there is a remarkable change of mood. Richard, the silly ruffian who had taunted an old man on his deathbed, becomes in defeat the image of a great man cast down. The delicate political situation required some literary acrobatics. The popular imagination identified Queen Elizabeth with Richard and Essex with Bolingbroke, and it was dangerous to commit oneself too completely to either. But Shakespeare went farther than was necessary. Exactly as he did in *Edward III,* he read into Richard the processes of his own elaborate and very curious mind. In the Dark Lady sonnets he had imagined himself the advocate of the Dark Lady and the Friend, pleading the case against himself, and in the same way Richard tells the rebels:

Nay, if I turn my eyes upon myself
I find myself a rebel with the rest.[2]

The identification is complete when we find Richard fascinated by the contradiction in terms that fascinated Shakespeare himself.

My brain I'll prove the female of my soul,
My soul the father: and these two beget
A generation of still-breeding thoughts;
And these same thoughts people this little world
In humours, like the people of this world
For no thought is contented. The better sort
(As thoughts of things divine) are intermixed
With scruples, and do set the Word itself
Against the Word.[3]

Setting the word itself against the word is, as I have said, a development of the simple conceit "Myself myself confound" and it is something much more than a mere literary ornament. It is its application to a psychological problem that gives *Richard II* its astonishing quality. In this play, from the critic's point of view, subject and treatment are never fully equated; the emotion portrayed has no full formal equivalent, and the blinding self-pity with which Richard is in-

[2] *Richard II,* IV. 1.
[3] *Richard II,* V. 5.

vested always transcends the dramatic content and spills over like honey from a pot. The abdication scene is not an abdication, but a crucifixion—and was so regarded by Shakespeare—and if the producer is not to embarrass an audience he must at any cost repress his principal actor.

The method here is crude; it is almost a theatrical confidence trick, but it comes off, and in doing so makes the rest of Elizabethan tragedy look like the hope of orphans and unfathered fruit. What it does in practice is to lower the key of tragedy by several pegs, as comedy lowers it in *Edward III*, and so bring tragic poetry within Shakespeare's lyric compass. One can immediately detect the difference in quality. This is verse in which the meaning of the words has been sifted, in which Shakespeare has "set the word itself against the word." No one really wants to know the meaning of the adjectives in lines like "The gaudy, blabbing and remorseful day" or "To find the empty, vast and wandering air" or "Of the old, feeble and day-weary sun." They are aimed at the midriff, not the head. It would seem as though Shakespeare had not yet reached the point of Mercutio's Queen Mab speech in *Romeo and Juliet* or Berowne's women-and-learning speech in *Love's Labour's Lost,* for their feathery, idiomatic, prosaic lightness of touch depends on a characterization that is still largely absent from *Richard II*. But one can see how the pitch has been lowered between

That raught at mountains with outstretched arms
Yet parted but the shadow with his hands

and Richard's speech as he looks in the mirror:

A brittle glory shineth in this face,
As brittle as the glory is the face.[4]

One can feel it again between the noble rhetoric of Warwick's dying speech in *3 Henry VI:*

My parks, my walks, my manors that I had
Even now forsake me, and of all my lands
Is nothing left me but my body's length [5]

and the pathos of Richard's speech with its tremulous repetitions, first indications of the mature style:

And my large kingdom for a little grave,
A little, little grave, an obscure grave.[6]

Probably one can see it best in the difference between two almost identical lines: one from *3 Henry VI,* the other from *Richard II.* When York is captured after the battle near Wakefield, Queen Margaret makes him stand on a molehill, wearing a paper crown, and thrusts into his hand a handkerchief steeped in his son's blood. "Now looks he like a king!" she snarls. When Richard II appears on the battlements of Flint Castle in defeat, York murmurs in almost identical words, "Yet looks he like a king."

One can feel the stereoscopic effect of the second line, the way in which it makes Richard stand out from his background and fills the stage with air and light. We are no longer suffocated by the claustrophobic

[4] *Richard II,* IV. 1.
[5] *3 Henry VI,* V. 2.
[6] *Richard II,* III. 3.

subjectivity of the Henry VI plays. The images are not as big, but they are in focus; the voice is not as powerful but it is in tune, and it is the sweetest voice in literature.

Why, having written two parts of the new historical sequence, Shakespeare interrupted it to write *King John,* or why he lingered years before resuming it, I cannot imagine, unless for all its delicacy *Richard II* was still too close to the historical knuckle. (When it was published in 1597 the abdication scene had to be omitted. It was produced by Shakespeare's company at the request of Essex' friends on the eve of their rebellion, apparently to rouse public feeling in favor of Elizabeth's deposition.) The theory that Shakespeare wrote *King John* to replace the uproariously anti-Catholic *Troublesome Reign* is probably correct. Professor Wilson argues that it is a revision made in 1594 of an earlier play, basing his conclusions mainly on a standing crux in the text. In III. 4. 68, King Philip's reference to Constance's disordered hair provokes her to reply in an even more disorderly manner "To England if you will." Both Professor Wilson and the Arden editor assume that this is an ironic reply to an earlier line of his "I prithee, lady, go away with me" and that what lies between is an interpolation, but in fact the line does not belong to Constance at all and it represents a simple typographical error. It is really the last line of the scene, Lewis' reply to the Cardinal's "For England, go!"

Professor Wilson also believes that Shakespeare worked on a prompt copy of *The Troublesome Reign of King John,* an old play of the Queen's Men, published in 1591, which he may have brought with him from the company. Shakespeare certainly did not work from a prompt copy, nor could he have been a member of the Queen's Men at any time when the play was in their repertory, for it is plain that he was as puzzled as Professor Wilson by it. The printed play contains two separate and mutually contradictory versions of the "discovery" of Philip the Bastard. Clearly this occurred during a revival of the play in which some well-known dramatist was invited to contribute a new and striking scene to attract fresh audiences. In the original version, placed second by the typesetter, Philip merely asked his mother:

Then, madam, thus; your ladyship sees well
How that my scandal grows by means of you
In that report hath rumoured up and down
I am a bastard and no Faulconbridge.

The revised version of this "discovery" scene, placed first by the typesetter, is one of the greatest things in English dramatic literature. In this the two Faulconbridge brothers, Philip the elder and Robert, are arrested for rioting, and, accompanied by their mother, are brought before King John and Queen Eleanor. Philip in his manly way refuses to plead in a matter concerning his mother's honor, but Robert proclaims him a bastard, incapable of inheriting the family estate. Asked who was Philip's father, Robert says that he believes him to have been Richard the Lion-Hearted. Richard spent much time at their home in the absence of his real father; Philip arrived *six* weeks before his time: his appearance answers for the rest. Angered by the charge against their famous kinsman, both the King and the Queen take Philip's side and declare that no proof has been offered. In spite of Robert's protests, the King decides that he will be satisfied by a mere declaration from Lady Faulconbridge and Philip. Lady Faulconbridge then takes an oath that Philip is her husband's rightful son. Philip himself begins to take an oath that he believes himself to be so, but, suddenly realizing the great blood he is forswearing, refuses to go on and abandons all claim on his inheritance. He is thereupon knighted by the King and accepted as Richard's son.

This magnificent scene, masterly in its writing, its timing, and its mounting tension, is quite complete in itself, but, as placed by the typesetter before the scene between Philip and his mother, it is certainly puzzling. Shakespeare, baffled by the inconsistency, and lacking a proper training on Shakespearean texts, assumed that Lady Faulconbridge's presence in the scene before the King and Queen must have been a mistake. Accordingly he deferred her entry until after the actual knighting, thus sacrificing the tremendous dramatic effect of her perjury. In her absence, the element of reasonable doubt which is the mainspring of the scene disappears, so he also altered the six weeks of the original to fourteen, which is absurd. For all the brilliance of his writing, he never for an instant gets within miles of the inspiration of his predecessor, whoever that may have been.

The weakness of *King John* is not that it is a mere chronicle play, but that, apart from Faulconbridge, it is not a very interesting one. Faulconbridge's part, however, is fascinating. Here—and also, I suspect, in the part of Berowne in *Love's Labour's Lost*—we have the beginning of a series of character parts written for an actor of extraordinary temperament with a considerable gift for mimicry. They range through Berowne, Faulconbridge, Mercutio, and Gratiano to the Hotspur of *Henry IV*. The type remains the same —the bluff, breezy, witty critic of worshipful society, the hater of ceremony and poetry talk, always with a contemporary extravagance spitted on his rapier's point. Here he is in *Love's Labour Lost:*

> *'A can carve too, and lisp: why, this is he*
> *That kissed his hand away in courtesy;*
> *This is the ape of form, Monsieur the nice*
> *That when he plays at tables chides the dice*
> *In honourable terms.*[7]

And here in *Romeo*:

> The pox of such antic, lisping, affecting fantasies, these new tuners of accents: 'by Jesu, a very good blade, a very tall man, a very good whore!' [8]

King John:

> *'My dear sir,'*
> *Thus leaning on my elbow I begin,*
> *'I shall beseech you'—this is Question now,*
> *And then comes Answer like an Absey book:*
> *'O sir,' says Answer, 'at your best command;*
> *At your employment, at your service, sir.'* [9]

[7] *L. L. L.*, V. 2.
[8] *R. and J.*, II. 4.
[9] *King John*, I. 1.

The Merchant of Venice:

> *There are a sort of men whose visages*
> *Do cream and mantle like a standing pond,*
> *And do a wilful stillness entertain*
> *With purpose to be dressed in an opinion*
> *Of wisdom, gravity, profound conceit,*
> *As who should say 'I am Sir Oracle,*
> *And when I ope my lips let no dog bark.'* [10]

1 Henry IV:

> Heart, you swear like a comfit-maker's wife! 'Not you in good sooth!' and 'As true as I live,' and 'As God shall mend me' and 'As sure as day.' [11]

It is with this character that we first get the Shakespearean soliloquy, a form which, so far as I know, is peculiar to Shakespeare. Usually it is only faintly dramatized, or—as in the Queen Mab speech or Hamlet's meditation on suicide—not dramatized at all. It corresponds to the Aristophanic parabasis, a personal appearance, a piece of simple essay writing, or a solo on whatever subject happened to interest the author at the time. I cannot help wondering whether the brilliant actor for whom these parts were written was not Shakespeare himself.

This is a part of his career of which we know little. The recorded traditions are worse than useless because they contradict the little we do know. That little consists of the actor lists for two plays by Ben Jonson,

[10] *M. of V.*, I. 1.
[11] *Henry IV*, III. 1.

Sejanus and *Every Man in His Humour*. As I find myself in complete disagreement with almost everybody who has written about these lists, let me reproduce them so that the reader can decide for himself. Here is the list for *Sejanus*:

Ric. Burbadge	Will. Shakespeare
Aug. Philips	Joh. Hemings
Will. Sly	Hen. Condel
Joh. Lowin	Alex. Cooke

"How big was his [Shakespeare's] part?" asks Mr. Ivor Brown in his book on Shakespeare. "The numbering suggests the fifth largest."

But now let the reader study the second actor list.

Will. Shakespeare	Ric. Burbadge
Aug. Philips	Joh. Hemings
Hen. Condel	Chr. Beeston
Will. Slye	Joh. Duke
Will. Kempe	

Whatever that list may suggest it cannot possibly suggest that Burbage, the idol of the Globe Theatre, played the *sixth* largest part. We do not know where Jonson got his actor lists from, and playbills of the period have all disappeared, but these lists strongly suggest playbills and must certainly be read as such—that is, across, not down.

It is quite plain that in *Every Man in His Humour* Shakespeare played the lead, probably Bobadill, while Burbadge played second lead, and that in *Sejanus* Burbadge played the title part while Shakespeare probably played Tiberius. It would seem from the lists that Burbadge and Shakespeare were the two stars of the

Globe, and from the alternation of leads I get the impression that Burbadge was principal tragedian, Shakespeare principal comedian. Besides, none of Burbadge's known successes was in comedy.

Dryden records the tradition that when an admirer asked Shakespeare why he had killed off Mercutio so soon, Shakespeare replied that he did it in order not to be killed himself. As a reply from the author of *Romeo and Juliet* this does not make much sense, which is probably why no one has paid attention to it. As a reply from the actor who played Mercutio it would be perfect.

Chapter 6

Masterpieces

WITH *Romeo and Juliet, A Midsummer Night's Dream,* and *The Merchant of Venice* we reach the period of the great masterpieces.

Romeo is a betwixt-and-between play, of a rather curious kind, which at one extreme approximates less to the lyrical plays than to the earlier *Richard III* and at the other even surpasses the maturity of *The Merchant of Venice.* The reason may be that it was revised more than once. Of the textual disturbance in at least two scenes I am not competent to judge, but it is obvious that between the first and second quarto there was some rewriting; the marriage scene has been entirely rewritten, and the dying Mercutio (probably rightly) has been shorn of some of his bitter puns: I regret the loss of his proposed epitaph—

Tybalt came and broke the Prince's laws
And Mercutio was slain for the first and second cause.

But the real test for literary man is the obviously archaic style of some scenes and the equally obvious mastery of others. Never did undergraduate so dreadfully display his ingenuity as Shakespeare does in the delighted dissection of lines like "Beautiful tyrant, fiend angelical"; "Come Montague for thou art early up to see thy son and heir now early down"; or the ghastly "This may flies do while I from this must fly." As in the Henry VI group we get the heaping up of useless words as in "Beguiled, divorcèd, wrongèd, spited, slain," and we seem "to hear the lamentations of poor Anne" in the Nurse's "O woe, O woeful, woeful, woeful day," which rivals anything in the dramatic line of Bottom the weaver. On the other hand, there is the infallible sign of maturity we find in the love scenes; the length of the poetic phrase. In Mercutio's Queen Mab speech, using only his half voice, Shakespeare can produce marvels of delicacy and sweetness, but no momentary inspiration could account for the faultless phrasing of the full concert voice.

O speak again, bright angel, for thou art
As glorious to this night being o'er my head,
As is a winged messenger of heaven
Unto the white-upturned wondering eyes
Of mortals that fall back to gaze on him
When he bestrides the lazy puffing clouds
And sails upon the bosom of the air.[1]

[1] *R. and J.*, II. 2.

I think that here, as certainly in *The Merchant of Venice,* the main influence on his work is Marlowe's. One whole scene in *The Merchant of Venice* is cribbed directly from *Tamburlaine.* Marlowe's "The moon sleeps with Endymion every day," becomes Portia's "Peace ho! the moon sleeps with Endymion." He has rid himself entirely of his fondness for choplogic, and, tired of the tight, trim, niggling verse he had been writing, tries for great splashes of color. In the other two plays of the group the vivid, incantatory classicisms of Marlowe throw a smoky torchlight upon the scene.

Did'st thou not lead him through the glimmering night
From Perigenia whom he ravished,
And make him with fair Aegles break his faith,
With Ariadne and Antiopa? [2]

Or—from *The Merchant of Venice*—

With no less presence but with much more love
Than young Alcides when he did redeem
The virgin tribute paid by howling Troy
To the sea-monster.[3]

Or, once more, from the same play—

In such a night
Stood Dido with a willow in her hand
Upon the wild sea-banks and waft her love
To come again to Carthage.[4]

[2] *M. N. D.*, I. 2.
[3] *M. of V.*, III. 2.
[4] *M. of V.*, V. 1.

Like all actors, Shakespeare had an uncannily retentive ear which could not only recollect a cadence but embalm an error. In *Soliman and Perseda,* which he must have played in in his younger days, there is a line about "Juno's goodly swans"—a mistake, for the swans are Venus', not Juno's—but he saved them up for *As You Like It*: "Like Juno's swans still we went coupled and inseparable." [5] He must have been a born mimic; he loves to break up his speeches with parody, and has a kind of chameleon quality which makes him seize on any opportunity for a change of style. Those who believe his works were written for him by Marlowe, Greene, Peele, Kyd, and Chapman, have plenty of stylistic grounds, for just as in *A Midsummer Night's Dream* he can cheerfully plunge into a parody of a group of village mummers, he can adapt himself to almost any style. At the same time, being a man of original genius, he never stays adapted.

Even in *The Merchant of Venice* he does not stay adapted. In the second act there is a scene between two garrulous Venetian merchants, Salarino and Salanio. They describe the frenzy of Shylock after Jessica's elopement in a passage clearly modeled on Marlowe's *Jew of Malta*—"O girl! O gold! O beauty! O my bliss!"

My daughter, O my ducats, O my daughter!
Fled with a Christian, O my Christian ducats! [6]

Then Salarino tells how on the previous day he had met a Frenchman

[5] *A. Y. L.*, I. 3.
[6] *M. of V.*, II. 8.

Who told me in the narrow seas that part
The French and English there miscarried
A vessel of our country richly fraught.

So far Marlowe's influence. But now we pass to the next scene but one, where again we meet the same two chatterboxes, but this time talking prose, and again we are informed that "Antonio hath a ship of rich lading wracked in the narrow seas; the Goodwins I think they call the place, a very dangerous flat and fatal, where the carcases of many a tall ship lie buried." Shylock appears and we get a characteristic Shakespearean scene of the period with its shattering repetitions—"a beggar that was used to come so smug on the mart—let him look to his bond! He was wont to call me usurer—let him look to his bond! He was wont to lend money for a Christian courtesy—let him look to his bond!" The chatterboxes go off, and to his fellow Jew, Tubal, Shylock bursts out in a terrific speech, and it is no longer a mere report of what has happened off stage, but the thing itself.

Why there, there, there, there, a diamond gone cost me two thousand ducats in Frankfort—the curse never fell on our nation till now; I never felt it till now—two thousand ducats in that and other precious, precious jewels: I would my daughter were dead at my foot and the jewels in her ear; would she were hearsed at my foot and the ducats in her coffin.[7]

Now, whether or not there was any interval between the writing of these two scenes, one does not have to

[7] *M. of V.*, III. 1.

be a literary critic to realize that they are the same scene, and that all Shakespeare has done is to take the hint contained in the Marlovian blank verse and expand it into the prose which by this time was becoming his favorite medium. They make an interesting contrast, for they show the direction in which he was moving. Though he might be lured into writing blank verse fantasy, his ultimate aim was a closer realism. He refused to stay adapted.

The part of Antonio is the last lingering echo of the Dark Lady episode. As Sir Edmund Chambers and others have pointed out, his melancholy is inexplicable unless we regard it as produced by Bassanio's forthcoming marriage. The melancholia broods over the play which has remarkably little cleverness. For the first and only time Shakespeare, in one dangerous line, says what Montaigne had already been saying in France—that tortured men will say anything. Was he thinking of Kyd, whose heartbroken preface to *Cornelia* he must have read?

But the most striking echo of the Dark Lady tangle escapes all the commentators. Bassanio has always been unpopular with them. He has no visible means of subsistence; he borrows money from Antonio, and his only notion of repairing his fortunes is by a wealthy marriage. What they have failed to note is that it is precisely his peculiar, half-loverlike relationship with Antonio which explains his fortune hunting. They see that Bassanio is a reflection of the young nobleman of the sonnets but they fail to see that this relationship of rank is also maintained in the play; and that an aristocrat in Bassanio's position could not have done otherwise than seek his fortune in marriage.

I think the distinction in rank has probably been somewhat obscured by rewriting. It is inevitably obscured for the modern reader and playgoer since he is entirely unaware of the light and shade represented for an Elizabethan by the changes rung on the formal second-person plural and the intimate second-person singular. As with ourselves and our use of Christian and surnames, the distinction was breaking down, but it never broke down to the point where a gardener called the lord of the manor by his first name or the mistress addressed the maid with the equivalent of "Miss Smith." Everyone in court must have known what Ralegh's fate was to be when Coke shouted, "I thou thee, thou traitor!" There are many episodes in Shakespeare where it is used with stunning effect, and whole scenes have lost their point by our modern inability to detect these changes of key. Half the fun of Malvolio's advances to Olivia is in the fact that he "thous" her; when Henry V dons Sir Thomas Erpingham's cloak to make his tour of the camp, his real disguise is not the cloak but the fact that even when "thoued" by Pistol he never forgets himself so far as to drop the formal "you"; when Falstaff accosts the young King on his procession through London his real offense is not that he claims intimacy with him but that he dares to "thou" him in public, which to any Elizabethan must have seemed like a capital offense. Here, I fancy, a foreigner could probably get more sense from Shakespeare than we can, for on the Continent this tradition is still very much alive.

There are two passages in *The Merchant of Venice* which reveal its significance. In the scene between Antonio and Bassanio the two friends use the formal "you" for the greater portion of the time. Then Bassanio mentions Portia, and it is as if a quiver of pain runs through Antonio. In his next speech he bursts out "Thou know'st that all my fortunes are at sea," and the whole scene becomes suffused with emotion. The second is the scene between Antonio and Shylock. Again Antonio uses the formal "you" until Shylock rates him for his anti-Semitism and Antonio snarls back "I am as like to call thee so again."

Anyone who reads the Belmont scenes with care will notice how Bassanio is addressed as "Your Honour," and though he "thous" Gratiano (a friend of Antonio's), is never "thoued" by him.

GRA.: My lord Bassanio and my gentle lady,
I wish you all the joy that you can wish,
For I am sure you can wish none from me:
And when Your Honours mean to solemnize
The bargain of your faith, I do beseech you
Even at that time I may be married too.
BASS.: With all my heart so thou can'st get a wife.
GRA.: I thank your Lordship, you have got me one.
My eyes, my Lord, can look as swift as yours.[8]

But Antonio is only one part of Shakespeare, the part that loved a lord. The other is Shylock. Shylock engaged the real contradiction in his nature, for he is the underdog out for revenge. Shakespeare takes great care to confine his aim to revenge. Though like Marlowe's Jew he is the villain of the play he is never allowed to say the sort of things Barabas says:

[8] *M. of V.*, III. 2.

As for myself, I walk abroad at night
And kill sick people groaning under walls:
Sometimes I go about and poison wells.

Undoubtedly, Shakespeare has taken great pains to see that he never becomes a really unsympathetic character: in us, as in Shakespeare, there is an underdog who has felt "the insolence of office and the spurns that patient merit of the unworthy takes," and we know what it is to desire revenge, even to the extreme of murder. Heine tells the story of the English girl who sat near him during a performance, and who at the trial scene burst out with "O, the poor man is wronged!" That, of course, is the risk which Shakespeare ran: Shylock, like Falstaff after him, is the secondary character who steals the play, which tends to turn into the tragedy of the innocent Jew wrongfully deprived of his hard-earned pound of flesh; and it takes the whole subplot of the rings, the serenade, and the music to restore the key of comedy.

The greatness of this very great play is that it searches out the Shylock in each of us, and makes us bring in a verdict against judgment and conscience. "The poor man is wronged."

Chapter 7

Falstaff and Hal

SHYLOCK IS DRAWN with careful realism, and, as in all the plays of the realistic period, Shakespeare tends to fall back on prose as the subtler instrument, a tendency even more marked in the two parts of *Henry IV*. But realism is a word we must use with great care. For seven or eight years Shakespeare conceived it his task as an artist to "hold as 'twere the mirror up to Nature," but he never understood realism as a mere copying of Nature. With him the reflecting medium, whether prose or verse, always came first. Character modifies and enriches it, but is never allowed to replace it, as it frequently does in modern realistic writing. That is to say, Falstaff, Shylock, Benedick, and Beatrice are encouraged to speak in their own way, always provided that it is not less striking than Shakespeare's way. "I will live in thy heart, die in thy lap and be buried in thy eyes; and moreover I will go with thee to thy uncle's." [1] The phrase is the important thing.

The realistic ambiguity of *The Merchant of Venice* is nothing to that of *Henry IV*. Prince Henry is a heroic figure drawn with such asperity that critics have accused him of insensibility; Falstaff a comic ruffian drawn with such lyric tenderness that he steals the play, and whole books have been written to deplore

[1] *M. A. N.*, V. 2.

the young King's shabby behavior in casting him off. "The poor man is wronged." One is glad to know that the balance is being redressed by Professor Wilson.

But surely, the important thing to remember is that there is a Falstaff in each of us, and that it is to this Falstaff that Shakespeare appeals. There was certainly a Falstaff in himself. Wherever in literature we find those great doubles: Quixote and Sancho, Bouvard and Pécuchet, Daedalus and Bloom, Morell and Marchbanks in Shaw's *Candida,* or Laevsky and Von Koren in Chekhov's *The Duel,* they are never different characters, but different aspects of the same character, usually the author's, and usually externalizing a conflict within himself.

When Hotspur cries "To pluck bright honour from the pale-faced moon!" and Falstaff gloomily asks "What is Honour?" Falstaff, as Dr. Harrison points out, is guying Hotspur, but even more, Shakespeare is guying Shakespeare. Realism is the artistic equivalent of logical thought, and while the poet in Shakespeare reveled in the thought of war, the realist, shrinking from its horrors, was bitterly conscious of the disparity between its causes and effects. One image in particular seems to have haunted him. "The soldiers," says Margaret, "should have tost me on their pikes"; the poor countryfolk of *Edward III* "fall numberless upon the soldiers' pikes," while Hippolyta in *The Two Noble Kinsmen* speaks of "babes broached on the lance." And so, in *Troilus and Cressida* we find the conflict between the young enthusiast, Troilus, and his elder brother, Hector, over Helen of Troy, whose "youth and freshness," in Troilus' lovely phrase, "wrinkles Apollo's and makes stale the morning," while to Hector she is merely "a thing not ours, nor worth to us, had it our name, the value of one ten." We find the same conflict in *Hamlet* between the firebrand, Fortinbras, and the philosopher, Hamlet, with his lament for "the imminent death of twenty thousand men, who for a fantasy, for a trick of fame, go to their graves like beds."

It is not only Falstaff who asks "What is Honour?" Shakespeare at the time was asking it too, and, distrusting romanticism, turning away from poetry to prose, and delighting in the bluff violence of his Mercutios and Hotspurs, was in the humor for guying any form of extravagance. In Pistol he indulges in a bout of malicious gibing at the heroic convention in poetry which reveals him in the Cervantes humor, and in the next play he went even further and invented Nym in order to have a fling at the academic realism of Chapman and Ben Jonson.

In *Henry IV* and *Henry V* there are two Englands, marvelously balanced; the one romantic, remote, medieval, the other realistic, intimate, prosaic; an England which starts off about its business at dawn with a good grouse at the inn. "They will allow us ne'er a jordan, and then we leak in your chimney, and your chamberlie breeds fleas like a loach." [2] Dramatically, it has little significance; it establishes only the atmosphere; the man awake behind the curtains of the big Tudor bed, watching the lantern flicker on the ceiling and listening to the rustic voices echoing under the wooden posts of the innyard. Scholars have pointed out how full these plays are of Cotswold names and places.

This balance, unerringly sustained throughout the

[2] *1 Henry IV*, II. 1.

first two plays, is magically symbolized in the third when the disguised King visits his troops on the night before Agincourt and learns their views of him. "As cold a night as 'tis he could wish himself in Thames up to the neck, and so I would he were and I by him." [3] Realism, which throughout the earlier plays performed the part of bass to the treble of poetry—Mercutio and the Nurse supporting Romeo and his sweetheart—in these plays sweeps up and drowns the note of the violins.

Just as Shylock speaks for the underdog in each of us, so Falstaff speaks for the average sensual man. In a modern play he would begin every second sentence with "As a matter of fact." The phrase which does identify him like a character in Dickens is "If I'm not speaking the truth, may I drop down dead!" and on this he continues to ring the changes till the carriers and even the Prince catch it from him, and we see how Shakespeare must have lived the part while writing the play, testing out every phrase with the intonation and gesture of the old man. "If I fought not with fifty of them, I am a bunch of radish: if there were not three and fifty upon poor old Jack, then am I no two-legged creature." [4] But like Robin Greene, of whom he frequently reminds me, he is a nonconformist preacher gone wrong; a man once much given to churchgoing and psalm-singing; and even at his worst he is still full of good resolutions, for tomorrow if not for tonight. "I must give over this life, and I will give it over; by the Lord, an' I do not, I am a villain." [5] But like the rest of us, he has been swearing the same thing off and

[3] *Henry V,* IV. 1.
[4] *1 Henry IV,* II. 4.
[5] *1 Henry IV,* I. 2.

on "any time this two and twenty years"; he does it to the familiar pattern of all his other asseverations, and when the Prince slyly asks where they shall take a purse next day, he instantly brightens up and says "Zounds, where thou wilt, lad; I'll make one; an' I do not, call me a vallain and baffle me." [6]

The great trilogy (for I regard *Henry V* as a third part of the play) is very uneven. The second part, which to judge from its abundance of legal allusions was written for performance at the Inns of Court, is already a decline, and *Henry V*, though it contains magnificent scenes, is a fiasco. Shakespeare must have been badly rattled when he wrote Falstaff's lines in the second part, for he gets nothing right. We scarcely hear the familiar peal of "An' I do not, call me a villain!" and not once does the old rascal swear to amend his ways. This may do very well for a substitute Falstaff, but it doesn't permit us to identify ourselves with the character—even the poor Civil Servant has hopes of salvation. Yet, inadequate as he may be, he is still a Hercules of a man, and his total disappearance brings down the curtain.

The mystery of his disappearance from *Henry V* has never been solved. Professor Wilson accepts the theory that the actor who played the part had left the theater, and identifies him with William Kempe, who certainly did leave the theater in 1599, the year when *Henry V* was produced, and whose name Professor Wilson thinks he recognizes in an entry for one "Will" in the Quarto of Part 2. From the parts Kempe is known to have acted, I do not see how he could have played the part of Falstaff, and the entry Professor Wilson relies

[6] *1 Henry IV*, I. 2.

on is clearly for the actor who played Dame Quickly. Dr. Harrison seems to think that Shakespeare had lost the knack of writing about Falstaff, and, seeing how much he had lost grip between the first and second parts, and between the second part and *The Merry Wives of Windsor,* this is a far more likely supposition.

With a purely instinctive writer like Shakespeare it is never safe to push such a question too far; he exhausted a subject or method with extraordinary rapidity, and then left the premises by the window; but my own belief is that he was compelled to drop Falstaff. There was certainly some censorship. Falstaff began as Sir John Oldcastle, but Shakespeare was forced to change the name. It is a reasonable assumption that Lord Cobham, whose family had intermarried with that of Oldcastle, was responsible, since Broome, the name adopted by Ford in *The Merry Wives of Windsor,* was originally "Brook" (the family name of the Cobhams), and Shakespeare was forced to change that too. Furthermore, while *Henry IV* was being performed by Shakespeare's company, a whitewashing play, *Sir John Oldcastle,* was produced by the rival theater, and largesse to the tune of ten shillings (say £5) was distributed among the authors, an item in Henslowe's accounts which always fills me with mild curiosity.

It is quite certain that Shakespeare conceived the plays as a trilogy with Falstaff accompanying the King to France, and that the scene in which the King casts him off, far from being the climax, as so many emotional commentators assume, is merely dramatic preparation for a reconciliation there, "where for anything I know," as the Epilogue says, "Falstaff shall die of a sweat, unless already 'a be killed with your hard opinions; for Oldcastle died a martyr and this is not the man." Curiously, Falstaff does die, and "of a sweat," but in England, not in France, and his death is merely reported, not shown on the stage.

I may be unduly suspicious, but to my mind there is something very fishy about all this. The impression I get from that magnificent and moving bit of reporting in which we are told of Falstaff's death is that his part in the third play had already been written, and that Shakespeare was compelled to cut it out. To me the words of the Epilogue "unless already 'a be killed with your hard opinions" suggest not an appeal for clemency, but, in conjunction with the following clause, "for Oldcastle died a martyr and this is not the man," a warning to the audience that their belief that Shakespeare had been attacking the memory of a Protestant martyr might make it impossible for him to continue the play as he intended.

Apparently it did, and because of it the play is a failure. "Banish not him thy Harry's company," old Falstaff had said, almost as though he already sniffed danger. "Banish not him thy Harry's company. Banish plump Jack and banish all the world!"

Chapter 8

Before *Hamlet*

IT WAS A PERIOD of serious change for Shakespeare Unless *Measure for Measure* (in an earlier form) intervened, *Much Ado About Nothing* must have been the last play he wrote for William Kempe. It seems to be a rewriting of an older play since the most important scene required by the scenario is entirely omitted —an unlikely event in a new play. Actually, the reason is that Shakespeare was finding it more and more difficult to adjust his mature realism to the demands made on it by the theatrical conventions of his day, grossly improbable from the realist's point of view, outrageously improper from the moralist's. The Elizabethan theater was a folk theater, and apart from Jonson's work remained so, and its influence constricted, while it enriched, an author's work.

The main plot of *Much Ado About Nothing* concerns a girl called Hero, engaged to a young man named Claudio. By some means, which in the play is never made quite clear, the villain, Don John, bastard brother of the Duke, arranges that on the night before the wedding Claudio shall apparently see Borachio enter Hero's bedroom. Next morning at the altar he repudiates her, and she is left in a swoon. Her family give her out for dead, and when Borachio is "reprehended" and the truth emerges, the repentant Claudio is persuaded by Hero's family to marry another girl, who of course turns out to be his own true love, returned from the dead.

The devices which Shakespeare resorts to so as to make this nonsense palatable are copybook craftsmanship. He attaches a subplot of his own devising about a cousin of Hero's, Beatrice, who is a shrew, and a friend of Claudio's, Benedick, who is a misogynist, and induces each to fall in love with the other through overhearing that the other is in love with him (or her). That is to say, he attaches a realistic subplot, which he writes for all he is worth, and, so far as a dramatist can, diverts the main drama into the new channel he has dug for it. We are not asked to share the highly improbable sentiments of a devoted family keeping Hero concealed; instead we are shown Beatrice eating her heart out with fury at the insult to her friend, egging on Benedick to kill *his* friend. Furthermore, by introducing the clowns as watchmen, and making them "reprehend" the "benefactor" of the bedroom plot while he tells an accomplice about it, Shakespeare succeeds in cutting out entirely the most embarrassing scene of the old romance; and by showing us the watch carrying out their investigations in their own enlightened way, he kids us gently along through a couple of enchanting scenes, almost unaware of the abysses of balderdash opening on either hand. It is a superb bit of craftsmanship, and, in spite of the gap in nature left by the missing *scène à faire,* it keeps the old comedy as fresh as a daisy.

At least half the play is carried by the clowns, and that is a risk which Shakespeare could never again have taken, for, in spite of the digs in the pirated version of *Hamlet,* Kempe must have been a fine artist. We seem to trace him from the first skimpy outlines in Costard and Launce to his apotheosis in Dogberry and Pompey Bum. He was obviously the type of melancholy clown who comes on the stage slowly, with his trousers hanging down, to take the audience into his confidence—in trouble again. He never sees the point of any remark, as his limited acquaintance with the English language causes him to misinterpret and misrepresent everything, and he jogs mournfully on through a series of misunderstandings and malapropisms, wrapped in an impenetrable cloud of conceit until the supreme moment when some misunderstanding no more spectacular than the last induces him to regard himself as insulted. Then his rage is magnificent:

> I am a wise fellow, and which is more, an officer, and which is more, a householder, and which is more, as pretty a piece of flesh as any is in Messina, and one that knows the Law, go to! and a rich fellow enough, go to! and a fellow that hath had losses, and one that hath two gowns, and everything handsome about him: bring him away! O that I had been writ down an ass! [1]

His sudden illuminations are one of his great joys, as when Costard exults in the delicate bawdry of his superiors or Launce flares up after the departure of Speed: "Now will he be swinged for reading my letter —an unmannerly slave that will thrust himself into secrets." [2]

But on the whole he is a warmhearted fellow, and full of sympathy for neighbors who lack the benefits of intellect which "Fortune" has showered on him. "Goodman Verges, sir, speaks a little off the matter, and old man, sir, and his wits are not so blunt as God help I would desire they were, but in faith, honest, as the skin between his brows." [3] "He is a marvellous good neighbor, faith, and a very good bowler: but for Alisander—alas, you see how 'tis—a little o'er-parted." [4]

He obviously set the key for all the low comedy parts in the earlier plays, for it is not only those clearly

[1] *M. A. N.*, IV. 2.
[2] *T. G. V.*, III. 1.
[3] *M. A. N.*, III. 5.
[4] *L. L. L.*, V. 2.

written for him like Costard, Bottom, Dogberry, and Pompey Bum which exploit his characteristics, but others like Mrs. Quickly which apparently were written for other actors. They help us to accept the limitations of a folk art like the Elizabethan theater because they are themselves so obviously folk types.

These parts form a startling contrast to those for Robert Armin who took Kempe's place in the theater in 1599. Armin was equally clearly the slick clown who bounces on to the stage with a hop, skip, and jump, and a merry cry of "Here we are again!" Jonson in *The Poetaster* gives us a partial and unflattering picture of him.

> Your fat fool . . . let him not beg rapiers nor scarves in his over-familiar playing face, nor roar out his barren bold jests, with a tormenting laughter, between drunk and dry. . . . Give him warning, admonition, to forsake his saucy, glavering grace, and his goggle eye: it does not become him, sirrah: tell him so.[5]

He had a good voice and could write his own songs. He had an absolute passion for the work of Shakespeare; not so much for the comedy parts, which he probably thought he could do better himself, but for the great tragic roles. Again it is the old story of the clown with the painted face who watches with jealous rage while Hamlet comes off, still list in the cloud of his passion. When ten years later Armin wrote a play himself, it was about a young man whose sensibilities were outraged by his mother's adultery (only apparent this time, one is glad to say). His name was

[5] *The Poetaster,* III. 4. 300.

Humil! That preposterous play of his, *The Two Maids of Mortlake,* is to me the most moving of all Shakespearean documents, for it reveals all that the historical documents conceal; the tremendous impact on the imaginations of simple men that was produced by Shakespeare's presence: it is like the splashing of waves on the shore after the great ship of literature has sailed silently by.

As You Like It (1599) was actually begun for Kempe, "the roynish clown," and hastily adapted for Armin. The play presented few difficulties except the usual one of the girl in boy's clothes, which never troubled Shakespeare since he hadn't seen a real actress. Rosalind is an enchanting bit of part-writing for the quick-tongued lad who played Beatrice: but apart from her the play is something of a rag bag. A part has been provided for a mysterious satirist called Jacques who has nothing at all to do and, like Pistol and Nym, seems to have been dragged in merely to ridicule some contemporary figure or extravagance. Shakespeare found it impossible to fit Armin in, and his part, like Jacques', remains outside the action and could be suppressed with little damage to the play. He has a mistress called Audrey, a rival called William, and a hedge parson called Oliver Martext to marry him, but his lines never rise above the level of deft patter, and they cast a cold deliberate light over the whole play which is absent from its weaker but more human predecessor.

I press in here, sir, amongst the rest of the country copulatives to swear and to forswear, according as marriage binds and blood breaks: a poor virgin, sir, an ill-favoured thing, sir, but mine own; a poor humour of mine, sir, to take that that no man else will: rich honesty dwells like a miser, sir, in a poor house, as your pearl in your foul oyster.[6]

The slick, bloodless, homosexual patter refuses to take dramatic coloring like Kempe's robuster buffoonery; nor did Shakespeare ever succeed in dramatizing it, for in *Twelfth Night* and *All's Well That Ends Well* Armin remains the court clown. Contrary to the usual view, I feel that the former play is again a decline on *As You Like It*. It is, of course, excellent theater, but the lyric quality is fitful and slight, and Armin's icy slickness invests all the characters in an impenetrable armor of allusiveness. The compositor probably added to this because I cannot help feeling that Sir Toby's "My lady's a Cataian; we are politicians" [7] does less than justice to Olivia's character; I fancy Shakespeare meant her to be a "Catonian" (i.e., My lady's a woman of principle; we are opportunists). The weakness is the weakness of all cleverness: the glassy surface, the lack of interior perspective. The epigrams, all to one tune, are rolled off suavely like those in a Wilde play, but though one thinks of the epigrams themselves one never thinks of who said them or in what connection. Gilbert ridiculed them neatly in his "I would as lief be thrust through a quicket hedge as cry Pooh to a callow throstle." Only in *Lear*, where the peculiarly eerie quality of cleverness gives it a kind of ghostly music, does Shakespeare get near dramatizing it. So far as I recollect, malapropism as a source of fun practically disappears from the plays, and its place is

[6] *A. Y. L.*, V. 4.
[7] *T. N.*, II. 3. 77.

taken by patter and repartee; and something of warmth, of kindness, of the poetry of the inn and the village green disappears with it. We no longer hear the music of "He is a marvellous good neighbour, faith, and a very good bowler." It is as though the lights were going out in Shakespeare's mind.

I feel that none of the plays of this period really comes off. *The Merry Wives of Windsor* is a good rough comedy but without a glimmer of distinction. The Fenton and Windsor Park scenes are in a distinctly un-Shakespearean style, and believers in the transmigration of plays have no difficulty in proving that the soul of his grandam inhabits Falstaff. I suggest that they may be the work of the man who wrote the couplets in *All's Well That End's Well* and that, instead of being the hypothetical author of "Old Plays," he may have been a scenarist who prepared the groundwork for this and other plays.

Julius Caesar (1599) is a very strange play in a very strange style. It is purely political and apparently intended to discourage would-be revolutionists by emphasizing the lesson of *Henry IV:* "An habitation giddy and unsure hath he that builds upon the vulgar heart." On that dubious text Shakespeare could preach till doomsday without a hint of unorthodox, let alone original, thinking: "preordinance and first decree," "the primogenitive and due of birth," "prerogative and tithe of knees" (the balance of Latin and English synonyms is characteristic of the period) never admit a rival, so that the play is necessarily satirical. In the scene of Mark Antony's speech the satire is brilliant, but satire dragged out for five acts is desperately tiresome, and, as if to emphasize this, it is written in a deplorable style. Sir Edmund Chambers, following Bradley, suggests that Shakespeare "was deliberately experimenting in a classical manner with an extreme simplicity of vocabulary and phrasing," which seems a rather inadequate description of the style to which he was condemned. The characters all tend to address one another and refer to themselves in the lachrymose third-person singular, a trick which Shakespeare with his idiomatic style used sparingly, and which reduces everything to the dead level of "Little Julie wants a doll." There is also a superfluity of auxiliary verbs and one wearies of learning how "I did mark how he did shake," while the oratorical repetitions make us far too conscious of the platform stage and of actors moving in a circle. At the same time, in other plays of the period Shakespeare does show a certain weakness for the third-person singular and for auxiliary verbs, even if to nothing like the same degree.

There are several signs that at this period Shakespeare was dissatisfied with his work and trying to escape from the folk drama. And there is little doubt that the principal influence making for this was Ben Jonson's. In the choice of two classical subjects like Julius Caesar and Troilus we have evidence that Shakespeare was seriously attempting to give his plays the classical unity and consistency of Jonson's. We know Jonson jeered at one line in *Julius Caesar,* "Caesar doth never wrong but with just cause"—which incidentally is perfectly correct—and we know Shakespeare got rid of it. Jonson was Joyce to Shakespeare's Yeats, the literary theorist as opposed to the natural instinctive writer, and might have said, as Joyce is supposed to have said to Yeats, "We have met too late; you are too old to be influenced by me," for, in spite of his experiments, Shakespeare remained a folk dramatist and—in his last plays—an obstinate and incorrigible one.

Still, *Troilus and Cressida* is a marvelous play, the first complete and consistent work of art Shakespeare had written in which even the antics of the clown have been fused with the main action. If, as I feel sure, Jonson instigated the high seriousness with which it is written, he is fully justified in it.

It has been variously interpreted as a comedy of disillusionment, an attack on Jonson and Marston, a warning to Essex, and a satire on Chapman's Homer, while some editors lean to the disbelief that Thersites represents Shakespeare's considered view of human existence as "Wars and lechery"—though not for long, one is glad to know.

There is, of course, something radically wrong with a play which leaves itself open to such a variety of misinterpretations, and we can accept it as proved. The main trouble is that for a play with such a title we see far too little of the lovers, and it looks far more like the first part of a history dealing with the fall of Troy. The main problem discussed is why Troy took so long to capture. Like all Shakespeare's political work it is tendentious and satirical, though the characters are much more clearly differentiated than in *Julius Caesar* and the political thought is on a far higher plane. The quotation from Aristotle, however anachronistic, shows that Shakespeare had picked up some of his ideas from that source. It is interesting to see Justice treated not as an absolute but as a mean between Wrong and Right; Choice as a mean between Will and Judgment; and—as in Nestor's warning that the success or failure of an elected representative has an important effect on the character of the community—the thought is sometimes profound. The language is a development of the stylistic experiment in the great choruses of *Henry V*. It may be that to write the French scenes in that play Shakespeare had started to read French again, because in quick succession he gives us a number of Gallicisms and semi-Gallicisms like "rivage," "sternage," "vaultage," and "farced." As well as this, he seems to have read some metaphysics, and between Gallicisms and Latinisms, the style of *Troilus and Cressida* frequently degenerates into mere jargon. There is wholesale coinage of words ending in "-ure" and "-ive": words like "flexure" and "tortive"; queer words like "mirable" and "convive"; and ugly words like "propugnation" and "oppugnancy"; and even Troilus is bound to become an unsymphathetic character when he tells us about

a credence in my heart
An esperance so obstinately strong.[8]

But the endur ing charm of the play is its suggestiveness. Few plays say less and suggest more. The use of the double plot is brilliant. The disillusionment of Troilus with Cressida is subtly and most movingly harmonized by the growing disillusionment of the warring armies whose great causes have begun to decline into mere personalities, vanities, and private attachments. Both armies are affected; the Trojans because though young Troilus, in love himself, believes that honor requires the retention of Helen, his maturer brothers, Hector and Helenus, remember the words of

[8] *T. C.*, V. 2.

Lucrece when she sees the strumpet Helen in the picture of Troy:

Why should the private pleasure of some one
Become the public plague of many moe?
Let sin, alone committed, light alone
Upon his head that hath transgressed so.[9]

But Shakespeare's main interest lay in the attackers. They are meeting with no success for the usual statutory reasons: "degree is shaked," "the odds is gone," "preordinance and first decree," "the primogenitive and due of birth," "prerogative and tithe of knees" are, as usual, in a shocking state. The statesmen are at loggerheads with the military leaders, and Shakespeare's treatment of the generals passes all the bounds of satire and becomes mere scurrility. Achilles and Ajax, the first with his effeminate friend Patroclus, are beasts and idots, who cannot be stirred except by appealing to their vanity and jealousy. Wise Ulysses sees that the only hope of getting Achilles to fight is to set up Ajax as a rival commander. The great plan meets with some success, but finally collapses when Hector refuses to fight Ajax on the ground that he is "his father's sister's son," while Achilles, subordinating his vanity to his lust, goes to keep an appointment with Polyxena in the enemy's camp! Here the irony is more reminiscent of Voltaire than Shakespeare.

It becomes even more blistering when the problem of the Greeks is settled not by the wisdom of Ulysses but by the thoughtlessness of Achilles' boy friend Patroclus, who gets himself killed by Hector while

[9] "Rape of Lucrece."

Ajax's friend loses his life at the hands of Troilus. At this point the generals decide that the thing is going too far and take the field. As Achilles is totally incapable of defeating Hector in fair fight, he has him murdered. This startling scene is the climax of the disillusionment in the underplot; the harmonic background to Cressida's betrayal of Troilus, which is murder on a different plane—the murder of the heart. The two themes are most ingeniously linked by the clown, Thersites, who is there as chorus on every occasion, even when Cressida is deceiving Troilus with Diomedes, and whose comments are always the same —"Wars and lechery! Still wars and lechery!" Editors ask incredulously, can this be Shakespeare? Of course, Thersites is a pure O'Casey figure—Shakespeare's reply to the libels of the liberal wits—and a satire on the satirists whose perpetual chorus of criticism in his view sapped the state. Ten years earlier, Gabriel Harvey had used Thersites as a symbol for the same thing, and Shakespeare may actually have been thinking of Harvey's words

> But Titius or rather Zoilus in his spiteful vein will so long flurt at Homer, and Thersites in his peevish moods so long fling at Agamemnon that they will become extremely odious and intolerable to all good learning and civil government; and in attempting to pull down or disgrace other without order, must needs finally overthrow themselves without relief.[10]

Apart from what appears to be a recollection of the Dark Lady episode, I see no personal disillusionment in the play; nothing which links it in my mind with the

[10] Harvey, *Four Letters.*

tragedies that follow. I cannot for the life of me see where Dr. Harrison gets a Troilus who is "lust-mad" or a Cressida who is "a whore." It is a play of the ice-brook's temper, cold and bright like a frosty day, and with none of the Nordic glooms and fogs of the tragedies.

A great deal of the suggestiveness which gives the play its beauty must have come from Shakespeare's realization that the subject itself was dynamite. When the principal object of a writer is to cover up his tracks, it is useless to try and identify contemporary allusions, but surely, at the end of the sixteenth century only a political innocent could have failed to draw a parallel between Ulysses and Nestor, Ajax and Achilles on the one hand and Cecil and Bacon, Essex and Ralegh on the other. I find it impossible to believe that any Elizabethan could have seen (if any Elizabethan *did* see) so vicious a caricature of the military leaders of the Grecian army without thinking of his own military leaders, one of whom, compared by his admirers with Achilles, as Dr. Harrison has shown, sulked in a way distinctly reminiscent of that hero; while the remarkable passage about Ullysses' intelligence service must, I feel, have pointed the analogy to any Londoner. If the play ever was produced, which is uncertain, it must have been when Achilles-Essex was already a doomed man.

This would fully explain its strange eventful history. On February 7, 1603, it was entered for publication by James Roberts "as it is acted by my Lord Chamberlain's men" but never published by him. In 1609 it was published by an entirely different publisher with a statement to the effect that it had never been produced at all. This proves that by that time it had been long dropped from the repertory, if it ever was really in it. What happened after February 7, 1603, which made it inadvisable either to publish or produce it, was clearly the Queen's death on March 24. Already, in the correspondence between Henry Howard, Earl of Northampton, and James VI, the destruction of Essex' enemies, Ralegh, Lord Cobham (who had apparently kicked up all the fuss about Falstaff), and Lord Grey de Wilton, was being prepared. On April 7 (I follow Dr. Harrison's admirable "Jacobean Journal") Cecil refused to allow Cobham to act as Ralegh's substitute Captain of the Guard. On April 10, Southampton and Neville, the two survivors of the Essex conspiracy, were released; on April 23, on his way south, James promised the Bishop of Durham, Toby Matthew, to restore the alienated property of his bishopric (Durham House, which Elizabeth had presented to Ralegh). On May 8, exactly one day after his arrival in London, James dismissed Ralegh from his position as Captain of the Guard; at some time before June 7 he ordered him to quit Durham House. On July 1, in the presence of the Queen, Southampton insulted Grey de Wilton during an argument about the Essex Rebellion. On July 14, Ralegh, Cobham, his brother, and Grey de Wilton were arrested on a charge of treason, Ralegh's treason being alleged to have taken place on June 9—long after a babe in arms might have seen he was due for destruction.

It was a bad time for enemies of Essex. Toward the end of May, Shakespeare's company produced Jonson's *Sejanus*. We have Jonson's own statement that "Northampton [Henry Howard] was his mortal enemy for brawling on a St. George's Day one of his attenders, he was called before the Council for his

'Sejanus' and accused both of popery and treason by him." The editors of the Oxford Jonson suggest that Howard, who was himself a Catholic, attempted to injure a coreligionist in order to conceal his own activities, but I am afraid that Jonson's statement is simply not true. The real reason why Howard hauled him before the Privy Council is revealed in a note by Dr. Harrison: "Ben Jonson, in the margin of his copy of Greenaway's translation of *The Annals* of Tacitus, noted opposite the account of the fall of Sejanus 'The Earl of Essex.' "[11] Jonson had already attacked Essex in *Cynthia's Revels* at a time when Essex no longer had any power. Howard was scarcely likely to forget that. In the following year Samuel Daniel was also haled before the Council for a slander on Essex. It was certainly not a good time for publishing a play like *Troilus and Cressida,* with all its echoes of the Essex conspiracy.

But apart altogether from this, some of the scenes are miracles of dramatic tact, of the deliberate refusal to underline a situation. We see early in the play that Hector wishes to send Helen back to her husband, Menelaus. Then Pandar, arranging for Troilus to spend the night with his niece, calls to Paris to make Troilus' excuses at supper; Helen makes fun of him; he goes, and Paris asks her to come and unbuckle Hector's armor. She agrees, and as they go out he suddenly throws his arms about her and murmurs, "Sweet, above thought I love thee." Not by a word has Shakespeare emphasized his fears that Hector may have his way. Remember, too, that unforgettable little scene I have mentioned already when the two brothers, Paris

[11] *A Companion to Shakespeare Studies,* p. 167.

and Troilus, the one the happy, the other the unhappy, lover, come to warn Cressida that she must leave the city. They utter just a few lines of verse which almost succeed in expressing the inexpressible. Last of all, consider the scene between Troilus and Hector on the morning of the final battle. Troilus has just had his own bitter experience of Cressida's falsity, Hector is going out to die by Achilles' treachery. By a supreme touch of dramatic irony, this is the moment when the lofty young idealist, Troilus, chooses to reprove his brother for showing pity to the vanquished.

HECTOR: Oh, 'tis fair play.
TROILUS: Fool's play, by Heaven, Hector.
HECTOR: How now! How now!
TROILUS: For the love of all the gods
Let's leave the hermit pity with our mothers,
And when we have our armours buckled on
The venomed vengeance ride upon our swords,
Spur them to ruthful work, rein them from ruth.
HECTOR: Fie, savage, fie!
TROILUS: Hector, then 'tis wars.[12]

The exploration of the mind of a romantic young man who has experienced his first disillusionment could go no further. And like everything else through this great play it is stated without comment, almost as though its implications had never occurred to the author.

Dramatic tact could go no further.

[12] *T. C.*, V. 3.

Chapter 9

Hamlet

THE REALISTIC PERIOD stops dead with *Hamlet* (1601-2), which is a play with two faces. One, with its delightful portrait of Polonius, as delicate as anything in Jane Austen, looks back to the lyrical plays; the other, with its gloomy soliloquies and the macabre humor of the Gravediggers' scene, written in for Armin, looks forward to *Othello* and *Lear*.

It is also a play of two styles. The first is smooth, lucid, and stately, its unit the couplet, or extensions of the couplet.

> *We do it wrong, being so majestical,*
> *To offer it the show of violence;*
> *For it is as the air invulnerable,*
> *And our vain blows malicious mockery.*[1]

The second is nervous, harsh, and vibrant, its unit the couplet between two half-lines.

> *O such a deed*
> *As from the body of contraction plucks*
> *The very soul, and sweet Religion makes*
> *A rhapsody of words;*
> *Heaven's face doth glow,*

[1] *Ham.*, I. 1.

Yea, this solidity and compound mass,
With tristful visage, as against the Doom,
Is thoughtsick at the act.[2]

"This solidity and compound mass" is one of the "dictionary" lines which identify the Shakespeare of the *Hamlet* period and after: it is a reversion to weight as against grace. The dictionary line, originally an ornament of early Tudor prose, became something of an obsession with Shakespeare. In *Henry V* (1599) he wrote " 'Tis no sinister nor no awkward claim," [3] than which no more sinister nor more awkward combination seems possible, but the twin of "sinister" haunted him for years until in *Sir Thomas More,* which must be at least five years later in date, he got in "To give the smooth and dexter way to me." [4] Frequently it is as though he *were* working with a dictionary, and testing both the Latin and English form of a word to see which was the better. "It is a nipping and an eager air." "The inaudible and noiseless foot of Time." "The primogenitive and due of birth." "The stroke and line of his great virtue." But sometimes with a nervous jerk he gives us not the translation but an apparently unrelated word which breaks the logical development with a snap and floods the line with pure association. "The expectancy and rose of the fair state."

There was an old play of *Hamlet,* probably by Kyd, but we can only guess what it was like. There is also a German *Hamlet,* unfortunately drastically cut, but whether this is derived from Kyd's or Shakespeare's

[2] *Ham.,* III. 4.
[3] *Henry V,* II. 4. 87.
[4] *Sir Thomas More,* III. 2.

play is hard to say. Sir Edmund Chambers believes it is merely a corruption of Shakespeare's.

Like Kyd's *Spanish Tragedy,* it opens with a Senecan prologue which is spoken by Night and the Furies. The first scene takes place on the battlements of Elsinore, and unlike *Hamlet,* in which the Ghost appears on two successive nights, the episode is closed in the first scene: the Ghost appears first to Horatio, then to Hamlet, to whom he recounts the story of his murder. Hamlet, interrupted by the Ghost while he tries to repeat the story to his companions, finally tells Horatio only, and explains that he intends to sham madness to get an opportunity of killing his uncle.

Laertes (here called Leonhard) is permitted to go to France while Hamlet is persuaded to remain at home. He first shams madness before Ophelia, and the King and Polonius (called Corambis) overhear the conversation in which he tells her to "go to a nunnery." The Players appear, and Hamlet, having given them some advice on acting, asks them to perform a play about the murder of King (he forgets the name) Pyr—Pyr—Pyrrhus. The Dumb Show only is performed; the King is shocked into betraying himself; Hamlet visits his mother's room and bids her "look upon this picture and on this," and kills Polonius who has been listening. He is sent to England, and Ophelia goes mad and makes bawdy overtures to a courtier. Hamlet, on his way to England, is attacked by two banditti, and kills both by dropping flat as they discharge their pistols at him. Laertes returns from France, demanding revenge, and Hamlet is killed with a foil poisoned by the King.

Besides this, we have also a shorthand version of

Shakespeare's *Hamlet* pirated by a printer. This is substantially like *Hamlet* as we know it, but there are two major differences. In this version, in which, as in the German, Polonius is called Corambis, the two scenes, Hamlet-Ophelia and Hamlet-Rosencrantz and Guildenstern, are transposed; and instead of the two scenes in which Horatio receives a letter from Hamlet and then discusses his escape with him, we have one scene only in which Horatio tells the Queen of his escape. Sir Edmund Chambers believes that both the German play and this derive from a performance of *Hamlet* in which, for some reason of prudence, "Polonius" was changed to "Corambis," and the two scenes, Hamlet-Ophelia and Hamlet-Rosencrantz and Guildenstern, were transposed, though he admits that "why the change should have been made is not clear."

The transposition of the two scenes might be accidental, though I think not. These shorthand piracies of popular plays were made under very difficult conditions, certainly by two men; sometimes, I suspect, by a teacher and his class. Each could write only for a few minutes without attracting attention, and though some of them were very indifferent reporters, their real problem was in fitting together the jig-saw of their separate notes into something resembling consecutive speech. Under such circumstances transposition was the rule, though not, so far as I can tell, transposition of whole scenes. The shorthand *Hamlet* is principally interesting because it sometimes preserves Shakespeare's words when he had forgotten them himself, as in "for he doth keep you *as an ape doth nuts,* in the corner of his jaw," and sometimes it gives us the actor's intonation as in "O your loves! your loves!—as mine to you."

To return to the German version. The only serious blot on it is the comic treatment of Ophelia's madness which is usually considered to be the work of the German adapter. I believe it to be the earliest of the three versions, merely because it is by far the most workmanlike scenario of the three, and I find it hard to imagine that a text can be clarified in corruption. Consider, for instance, the simple matter of the Ghost's repeated "Swear!" I do not think I am abnormally dense, but until I read the German text I had always taken that for a piece of romantic color, and never understood that the Ghost was uneasy at the thought of strangers learning the secret of his murder; that Hamlet broke off on his account, but merely deferred repeating the story till later. Of course, from the fact that at the time of the Play Scene Horatio knows the story, we may deduce that Hamlet told him, but why he delayed in telling him is certainly not clear from the play. One line in the German makes the whole thing plain. "The spirit of my father is perturbed that I should make this matter known."

Again, the scene of Hamlet's escape from his would-be murderers, however crudely it is treated, is a necessary scene which Shakespeare dropped to his own great confusion. He made two shots at covering up its absence, neither successful. It is not good craftsmanship to make the audience aware of a plot against your hero's life and then bring him back a quarter of an hour later to tell how he escaped it. It is bad craftsmanship when, as in *Hamlet,* the burial of Ophelia has to take place before he can tell the story at all, for by that time Hamlet's existence is taken for granted, and nobody gives a button how he escaped. The much-discussed question of whether or not the King saw the

Dumb Show is answered in a rather remarkable way, for it seems that the King saw nothing else. The whole story is simple and clear with none of the redundancies and inconsistencies of Shakespeare's play, though exactly how far this may be accounted for by cutting is not clear. There are no Rosencrantz and Guildenstern, no Marcellus, no Fortinbras, except in a casual reference, no gravediggers, no Hecuba scene—nor, indeed, is there any apparent need for them. The story is pure Deadwood Dick. Perhaps Shakespeare's most miraculous achievement was to take a Deadwood Dick story, which the audience knew as well as he did, and transform it into one of the great myths of the world.

His method—unsatisfactory from the artistic point of view—was to shift the emphasis. Hamlet of the German play is a Renaissance man of action, bold and cunning; and both the boldness and cunning have left their traces on *Hamlet,* notably in the scene where Hamlet apologizes to Laertes almost entirely in the third person singular (as suspicious here as in *Julius Caesar*) and excuses himself on the ground of his supposed madness. Sham madness as a dramatic convention was already as dead as Queen Anne—Shakespeare's Queen Anne. "It may appear to some ridiculous," [5] says the sham madman in Webster's play, with a nervous glance at the young gentlemen from the Inns of Court. Shakespeare's Hamlet is an intellectual afflicted with melancholia; so that even if there were no Rosencrantz and Guildenstern in the original play (and I see no reason to think there were), one can see how necessary it would have been to invent

[5] *The White Devil,* IV, 2.

them, merely to balance the sham madness which Hamlet assumes before Ophelia and Polonius with the real melancholy which Shakespeare was now trying to graft on him. Notice in particular how before the mad scene with Ophelia he interpolated the great meditation on suicide—clearly interpolated it, because, contrary to the convention of Elizabethan playwriting, the King and Polonius overhear the scene with Ophelia but not the soliloquy. And if you assume as I do that the German version is the earliest of the three, you can see exactly why it was that between the pirated version of 1603 and the official version of 1604, Shakespeare found it so necessary to transpose the Hamlet-Ophelia and the Hamlet-Rosencrantz and Guildenstern scenes—to correct any false impression and present his audience first with a Hamlet suffering from real melancholia rather than with one shamming madness.

The fundamental inconsistency between the scenario and the treatment is the cause of almost all the muddle in the play. Forgetting the limitations of his Deadwood Dick theme, Shakespeare tends to throw the emphasis too much on the intellectual side, and then is brought up dead by the limitations of the plot. The introduction of Rosencrantz and Guildenstern involves him in a typical difficulty. In the German version the whole thing is plain sailing; the players are strolling mummers; they appear, Hamlet instantly gets the idea of the Play Scene and gives them a lecture on acting. But then Shakespeare had the inspiration for the mighty Hecuba scene—probably from the same sources as so many other things in *Hamlet*—Montaigne's Essays—for, according to Montaigne,

Quintilian relates that he saw actors who entered so deeply into a tragic part that they still wept after reaching home; and of himself he tells us that having undertaken to work upon others' feelings he was so carried away by his own that he detected himself not only in tears but with the paleness of countenance and behaviour of a man really overwhelmed with grief.[6]

Accordingly, for the purposes of the scene, the mummers become the tragedians of the city (and perish any mummer who adopts Dr. Harrison's suggestion that the scene should be clowned!), on tour because of the vogue of child actors, and encountered on their way by Rosencrantz and Guildenstern. Now, Hamlet's advice to the players is merely in the way of the great scene, so, like the mad scene with Ophelia, it has to be pushed back to its present position; but even this doesn't entirely solve Shakespeare's problem, since with Rosencrantz, Guildenstern, and Polonius on the stage, it is impossible for Hamlet to arrange the details of the plot for making the King betray himself—yet, if he doesn't, he leaves the players with no dramatic carry-over. So in spite of the presence of the others Hamlet calls the chief Player aside and slips in a few lines about an imaginary speech which he is to write for the play next evening, and to this speech Shakespeare skillfully pegs the now homeless and destitute advice to the players. And even this leaves a very awkward moment, for the emotional effect of the Hecuba scene compels Shakespeare to follow up at once with the great monologue on irresolution and reserve the actual detail of the plot, which in the German play

[6] *Montaigne's Essays,* tr. Trechman.

precedes the Players' entrance, for the very end of the scene. Only the very suspicious notice that Hamlet has arranged for the speech which he is to write into the play before the idea of the Play Scene occurs to him at all. Shakespeare makes the same mistake as when he allows Hamlet to explain his escape after the burial of Ophelia, and for the same reason; that he has interpolated something into the text. It is exceedingly skillful but patchy.

I do not suggest that all the alterations were made at different times; they may represent no more than the ordinary changes of intention visible in the manuscripts of most writers; but some were certainly made between the appearance of the two Quartos, in 1603 and 1604, and I have a strong feeling that the whole mysterious Fortinbras business may be an interpolation connected with the old Queen's death and the problem of the succession.

Just consider how it is dragged in. In the very first scene Marcellus asks what is afoot in Denmark, and Horatio (elsewhere referred to as a stranger) explains in a long speech that a Norwegian prince called Fortinbras is raising an army to invade Denmark. Fortinbras appears again a few scenes later when two ambassadors, who have no other earthly business in the play, are dispatched to Norway to protest. Later they return with the information that Fortinbras *had* intended to invade Denmark, but that the King of Norway has now persuaded him to invade Poland instead. Will the Danes object to his crossing Danish territory with an army? No, the Danes have no objection, so Fortinbras makes another appearance, this time on his way to Poland with his army, and Shakespeare makes a gallant attempt to anchor him in the play, as he had already anchored the Hecuba scene, by contrasting Fortinbras' resolution with Hamlet's weakness. Nor is this all. At the precise moment when Hamlet has been stabbed with the poisoned foil, he and his army return, and, hearing him approach, Hamlet, who has been dying in a cloud of the most exquisite poetry, sits up to give him his vote for the succession to the throne.

This is absurd enough for anything, but we reach craziness when Fortinbras, without asking anyone's leave, announces that he proposes to annex Denmark anyway, and Horatio, forgetting all about his dead friend, hurriedly begs him to do it quickly before anyone can anticipate him—

Even while men's minds are wild, lest some mischance
On plots, and errors happen.[7]

This is the point in his work where Shakespeare's anxiety about the future becomes almost hysterical. He had written immediately before it two other plays both dealing with the danger of internal dissension and revolution. We know that *Hamlet* was produced at Oxford and Cambridge; I am inclined to share Sir Edmund Chambers' view that *Troilus and Cressida* was produced there, and I feel sure that the gagging passages between Hamlet and Polonius refer to a similar occasion.

HAM: You played once i' th' university, you say? . .
POL: I did enact Julius Caesar; I was killed i' the
 Capitol: Brutus killed me.

[7] *Ham.*, V. 1.

HAM: It was a brute part of him to kill so capital a calf.[8]

I can make nothing of this unless I assume that Polonius was played by the fat comedian who also took the parts of Sir Toby and Falstaff—"the fatted calf"—and that he also played Caesar ("let me have men about me that are fat") to Burbadge's Brutus at a university production. I should guess that the fat comedian was Heminges, and that there is another private joke in Sir Toby's "We are politicians." Heminges *was* "politician" or spokesman, of the company.

You may notice, besides, how Rosencrantz and Guildenstern expatiate on the dangers attending "the cease of majesty" [9] and how Laertes arrives on the scene accompanied by a mob howling "Laertes shall be king! Laertes king!" [10] You may notice the prosaic solder with which the Fortinbras scenes are joined in, such as "I think it be no other but e'en so" and "this business is very well ended," and perhaps agree with me that the date of those passages is probably the winter of 1602-3 when the old Queeen lay dying and Cecil was trying to prepare public opinion for the accession of a most unpopular and unpleasant foreign prince, who, like Fortinbras, had in his time sketched invasions on the English border. It may be too much to assume that behind the tendentiousness of *Troilus and Cressida* and *Hamlet* was a certain understanding between Cecil and Shakespeare, but it certainly seems strange that one of James' first public acts on reaching London was to appoint Shakespeare's company his

[8] *Ham.*, III. 2.
[9] *Ham.*, III. 3.
[10] *Ham.*, IV. 5.

personal players with the rank of Grooms of the Chamber.

Shakespeare is never a critical, consistent writer, as Jonson is, and nowhere was his consistency so sorely tested as in *Hamlet,* for his view of life seems to have been darkening even as he worked over it. In his early plays and poems the attitude to death was a simple contradiction in terms—"Death is the end of Death" —but from the moment Hamlet begins his meditation on suicide—a subject which was afterward never very far from Shakespeare's thought—we know that it has no vestige of connection with the play; that it has been spatchcocked into the scene where it stands; that it is not the ghost-ridden Hamlet who speaks of "the un-discovered country from whose bourne no traveller returns" or the heir to the throne who has felt "the insolence of office and the spurns that patient merit of the unworthy takes"; in fact, they have been gummed by a glaring *non sequitur* to the end of a speech on ir-resolution. We know that this, like the sonnets, and Audley's speech before Poiters, and Richard's in pris-on, is personal poetry, and that a shadow has come over Shakespeare's mind. He was so obsessed by suicide that, though Ophelia's death is a mere accident, she is buried as though she *had* been a suicide. The Play Scene, with its delightful air of parody, and the high comedy of Polonius give place to this and to the graveyard scene for Armin and his zany in which for the first time we find Shakespeare indulging a passion for macabre humor. In the graveyard scene there is a horror of the charnel house, stifled until the present moment, which would yet frame the pathetic inscrip-tion on his grave.

It is futile to speculate on the precise occasion of this melancholia. It may have been a dangerous illness. He was absent from the cast of a Jonson play in 1600. And it is interesting that Dr. Caroline Spurgeon has noticed in *Hamlet* the prevalence of images dealing with internal tumors; [11] but this, at the best, can be only guesswork. What we can do is put our finger on passage after passage which seems to echo the work of Montaigne; his acrophobia in "the cliff that beetles o'er his base"; [12] his views on fashions in handwriting in "I once did hold it as our Statists do a baseness to write fair"; [13] his quotation of Quintilian in the Player's tears; Etienne de la Boétie's phrase on death " 'Tis coming or 'tis past but present never" in "If it be now 'tis not to come, if it be not to come it will be now;" [14] most of all perhaps in that terrible phrase which Shakespeare was later to versify in *Lear* and *Cymbeline*—"I believe that which Plato says to be true that man was made by the gods to sport and play withal."

Atheism was no new thing in Elizabethan England. Ralegh, Chapman, Harriot, Marlowe, and Kyd were probably all freethinkers, but theirs was not the sort of disbelief which would have been likely to affect Shakespeare. Marlowe's atheism is that of the outlaw; it is antisocial rather than antireligious, and Shakespeare was never antisocial. Montaigne's was the first compendium of classical philosophy which Shakespeare could have read, and he was a rationalist who did not leave one shred of traditional belief in the

[11] Spurgeon, *Shakespeare's Imagery*.
[12] *Ham.*, I. 4.
[13] *Ham.*, V. 2.
[14] *Ham.*, V. 2.

mind of a sympathetic reader; nothing but that sense of the utter futility of human existence by which Hamlet is haunted.

At bottom rationalism and realism are aspects of the same frame of mind and, sooner or later, both are bound to come up against the supreme test of the irrationality of the universe. All classical civilization is summed up in that line of Sophocles, "Never to have lived were best," or Madame de Sévigné's thought that the best of all fates had been to die in her nurse's arms, or Housman's "O it was well with me in days ere I was born." No rationalism which fails to allow for a missing sense in humanity can escape it. For more than ten years Shakespeare had given himself to the view that the business of the artist was "to hold as 'twere a mirror up to Nature," and he was at the age when a realist who thinks at all is bound to ask himself if reality itself be real. I see no reason to suppose that any personal disillusionment such as the infidelity of a second Dark Lady caused the change in him. On the contrary, I feel that any explanation of that sort is not adequate to explain the change, and, given his genius, I do not see how he could possibly have escaped a religious crisis; or how the marvels of the imaginative universe which he had created could have failed to throw him back on the thought of his own extinction.

"Even the powerful mind of Johnson seemed foiled by futurity," Boswell tells us, and the meditation on suicide expresses the horror of that shuddering sensibility before "the Great Doom's image." It sets the key for Claudio's "Ay, but to die, and go we know not where," [15] and the Gaoler's "for look you, sir, you

[15] *M. for M.*, III. 1.

know not which way you shall go,"[16] and it is the very dizziness of the realistic height from which Shakespeare views it which gives him the tendency toward suicide, that longing to plunge at once into the abyss, "to rush into the secret house of Death" and "encounter Darkness like a bride and hug her in my arms!"—a strange distorted memory of Chapman's great line on the marriage night—

> *Fear fills the chamber, darkness decks the bride.*[17]

After *Hamlet* the attitude to death is perceptibly different. Shakespeare is no longer satisfied with the contradiction in terms, which he uses only once, and that in *Measure for Measure,* a play that seems as though it had existed in an earlier form. There is the revulsion against what to the rationalist appears to be the end of all, and then (merely because if it *is* the end of all, life itself is meaningless and we can merely shrink from its murderous claws) he is driven back upon death as the only thing "which shackles accident and bolts up change" and sings its praises. Again and again we hear this contradiction set forth, and grow accustomed, first to the spasm of revulsion, and then the constrained celebration of the only power which can quit us of the contradictions, the burnings and freezings—

> *Fear no more the heat o' the sun,*
> *Nor the furious winter's rages.*[18]

[16] *Cym.,* V. 4.
[17] "Hero and Leander."
[18] *Cym.,* IV. 2.

It is the presence of this new attitude to death which gives *Hamlet* its dual nature. In Polonius the antithesis is still open; there is still "I" and "you," but in the shuddering sensibility of Hamlet's reproaches to his mother and the morbid humor of the graveyard scene the jaws of the antithesis begin to close, and we revert to the Shakespeare of *Henry VI* and a drama which takes place only in the theatre of the poet's mind.

But what a difference there is in that mind!

Chapter 10

The Breakthrough

OTHELLO is the first play in which the excess of personal emotion which we notice in *Hamlet* is allowed to swing the action, and in *Lear* it rages like a storm. These two plays are among the greatest dramatic poems in the world; they are the work of a theater man whose skill is almost supernatural; yet they seem to me failures.

First of all, we must dismiss the idle speculation which finds in Othello's jealousy a key to Shakespeare's gloom. The flightiness of Cressida, the facility of Hamlet's mother, the doubts of Desdemona's virtue, do not mean that Shakespeare had met with another Dark Lady. They are part of a general abandonment of human values, aspects of a despair with human existence which can only be described as misanthropy.

The technical trouble with *Othello* is that it is high tragedy based on the scenario of a comic opera. It is not improved by Shakespeare's treatment, for in the original story Iago had been in love with Desdemona himself; excellent motivation, had he chosen to use it, but he did not, and left Iago, like Richard III, a mere inexplicable figure of evil. The handkerchief is a motif from court comedy, Portia's ring all over again, and quite insufficient to support the weight of the tragedy he builds on it. The scene in which Othello overlooks a meeting between Iago and Cassio and translates Cassio's gestures and laughter into a comment on his supposed affair with Desdemona is another and cruder example. In court comedy it is possible that it might pass muster in a bit of good-humored extravagance, but the convention is farcical, not tragic. The curious staginess of these tragedies reminds us of Hardy's novels, and the purpose seems to be the same. Shakespeare puts the Almighty on trial for murder and then fakes the evidence. Now, it is the essence of high tragedy that the more demands the author makes on our emotions, the more he will concede to our intelligence; the higher he keys his tragedy and flings his scepter at the injurious gods, the more he will try to convince us, as Sophocles and Racine do, that his statements are true and his conclusions inescapable, and that is the test *Othello* will not stand up to. There is more of the inescapable feeling of high tragedy in the scene from *Troilus and Cressida* in which Ulysses and Troilus overhear the love-making of Diomedes and Cressida than in anything in *Othello* up to the actual climax.

At the same time it would be foolish not to appreciate the way in which the abandonment of realism, the bursting of the dikes, releases a flood of passion and poetry. Undoubtedly, for years the poet in Shakespeare had been half strangled by his theoretical realism; the filter of human beings through whom it had to pass before reaching the audience had let through only a trickle from the vast reservoir of his imagination. Now it tears out, inundating and fertilizing great tracts of country. The moment the wretched machinery which precipitates the crisis has served its purpose, the play leaps on to a new plane.

One can see it best in the astonishing silences and half silences of the text. There are the stunned repetitions. "He echoes me as if there were some monster in his thought too hideous to be shown."

OTHELLO: Thy husband knew it all.
EMILIA: My husband.
OTHELLO: Thy husband.
EMILIA: That she was false to wedlock?
OTHELLO: Ay, with Cassio. . . .
EMILIA: My husband.
OTHELLO: Ay, 'twas he that told me first:
  An honest man he is, and hates the slime
  That sticks on filthy deeds.
EMILIA: My husband! [1]

Time and again it is as though the mind were so stunned that it could not respond, and then it leaps out in blazing hypersensibility, too vivid to remain for long upon the level of conscious thought and diving back into itself again so that we are bewildered by its responses. "And good lieutenant, I think you think I love you?" says Iago. "I have well approved it, sir," replies Cassio. "I drunk!" And there is Othello's:

[1] *Oth.*, V. 2.

Sir, she can turn and turn, and yet go on,
And turn again; and she can weep, sir, weep;
And she's obedient as you say, obedient,
Very obedient. Proceed you in your tears.
Concerning this, sir—O well-painted passison!—
I am commanded home. Get you away;
I'll send for you anon. Sir, I obey. . . .[2]

But the fundamental weakness of the play is simply that it is not interesting. In tragedy we know what the end must be, but the dramatic interest is in the details of the fight between destiny and a character not unmatched with it; the way in which destiny is foiled and recovers; in which the original simple doom is thwarted. But in *Othello* there is no fight, and there is no dramatic interest in watching through round after round the suffering of someone who cannot hit back, and Othello, Desdemona, and Cassio are all passive figures, and the only active figure in the play is an abstraction. If Iago, after playing the trick of the handkerchief had realized the danger in which he had involved himself by goading Othello too far, if then in terror he had set about trying to avert the inevitable catastrophe, we should have had drama and Othello would have ceased to be a passive figure, but I do not think that such a scenario would have satisfied Shakespeare at all. He was not interested in tragedy as such; he was interested only in saying what he had to say, and Iago, the puppet, was the only medium through which he could say it.

The same is true of *King Lear*. Even as a child I al-

[2] *Oth.*, IV. 1.

ways found it impossible to stomach the first scene in this play, and had the feeling, fatal to the appreciation of tragedy, "the man's a fool." A king divides his kingdom up among his three daughters, and then disinherits the favorite for refusing to join in a competition of flattery. Kent, the honest courtier who has defended her, is exiled. That opening scene would damn any play. But as it was part of his source material, we had better pass it and see what Shakespeare added to it. The King's follower, Gloucester, then disinherits and banishes his son, Edgar, on the unsupported allegations of his natural son, Edmund, and we are presented with a double plot involving two baneful and deluded old fathers, two sets of wicked children, and two sets of dutiful ones. Kent returns to the King's service in disguise in time to see Lear's wicked children drive him from their homes, insane, while Gloucester's son, Edmund, conspires with them to murder his own father. Regan and her husband between them tear out the old man's eyes. The two dutiful children set about restoring the balance. Edgar, pretending to be a madman—"it may appear to some ridiculous"—to escape his father's vengeance, meets the old man with his eye sockets still bleeding after his mutilation. He wants to commit suicide and asks Edgar to lead him to a certain high cliff. Instead, Edgar leads him to a hillock which he describes as a huge cliff, and the old man hurls himself off it, and is of course uninjured. Then Edgar comes up, this time in his proper person, and persuades his father that the hillock really had been a cliff, his guide a fiend trying to lure him to destruction, his escape a miracle. Then he goes out to challenge his wicked brother who, with his last dying kick, orders the hanging of Cordelia.

Now, seriously, what are we to make of this tissue of nonsense masquerading as tragedy? There is something dreadfully wrong with that particular scene between Edgar and his father. The playwright may show his hand too soon—the beginner's mistake—or too late—the journeyman's. If Shakespeare really was responsible for the scenario of *Lear* he shows it too late. The moment is past when we can be moved by the meeting between the deluded father and his wronged son, and no tragic dramatist in his right mind would ever deliberately have sacrificed such a scene merely to extract another rabbit from the dramatic hat. There is a second example of a delayed climax at the end of *Measure for Measure* which is even clumsier.

In the presence of a crude collaborator we may, if we choose, bring in a verdict of "not proven" regarding the bloodthirsty tomfoolery of Barnardine and Roggazine in *Measure for Measure,* and the bringing in of Macbeth's head on a pole but we cannot acquit Shakespeare of the same sort of tomfoolery over Cloten's body in *Cymbeline* or the stamping out of Gloucester's eyes in *Lear*. They are part of the psychological wantonness of which the later plays are full. When Shakespeare opened the dikes, something more than poetry came in. Cymbeline banishes Posthumus in a childish frenzy like Lear's or Gloucester's, Posthumus, himself banished, in a childish frenzy like Othello's, believes some nonsense about Imogen's fidelity and orders her murdered. *A Winter's Tale* opens with a king who, for no particular reason, imagines that his wife has deceived him with Polixenes, and orders the murder of Polixenes, the trial of his wife, and first the burning and then abandonment of his newborn baby

Perdita. (In this welter of neuroticism it is merely a detail that the kind old courtier who is compelled to expose her is eaten by a bear—presumably Shakespeare's company *had* a bear.) Perdita in turn falls in love with Polixenes' son, whereupon Polixenes orders the execution of her supposed father and the banishment of everybody. And even stranger than the phantasmagoria of men mad with jealousy and power is the fantasy of girls with pretty-pretty names—Cordelia, Perdita, Miranda, and Imogen; the passive principle opposed to the active one. There is no trace of the ambiguity which defines the characters of Richard II, Shylock, or Falstaff. Nothing opposes the storm of misanthropy which blows through these later plays, and we can hardly escape the feeling that the image of the burst seed pod which we find for the first time in *Lear* and again in *Macbeth, Timon of Athens,* and *A Winter's Tale,* represents Shakespeare's own thought.

> *Crack Nature's moulds, all germens spill at once*
> *That make ungrateful man.*[3]

The misanthropy is, of course, common to other writers. European civilization, as reintroduced by James I, had some features which must have appeared unfamiliar to Englishmen. Thanks to their virtual isolation during Elizabeth's long reign they were in some ways far ahead of their contemporaries on the Continent, but generally far behind. The Renaissance had influenced them deeply, but they were still medieval, almost Catholic in outlook; and this came out whenever they tried to express themselves in architecture,

[3] *Lear,* III. 2.

prose, or drama. The Elizabethan theater with its canopied stage, half a picture stage, half a platform set up in an innyard, is typically transitional in character; something which must change immediately. The typical Tudor building, full of memories of Gothic and rumors of the Renaissance, is merely a temporary compromise.

Elizabeth, as wise as James was foolish, realized that absolute monarchy in a country politically as mature as England was a risky business, and for a woman it might have been fatal. She steered a clever middle course, ruling as she said (not altogether insincerely) by her people's love. Middle-class opinion counted for a good deal. Shakespeare and his company were still what the middle classes considered them: rogues and vagabonds. One of James' first acts was to make them Grooms of the Chamber. "Kings," he explained, "are not only God's lieutenants upon earth and sit upon God's throne, but even by God himself they are called gods." Shakespeare versified it in *Sir Thomas More,* a play by a team of writers, into which he wrote two scenes, probably about 1603-4, and one of which some famous scholars believe is in his own handwriting.

[God] hath not only lent the King His figure,
His throne and sword, but given him His own name,
Calls him a god on earth.[4]

"I think the King is but a man as I am," said the disguised Henry on the night before Agincourt, and here Shakespeare was expressing the humane and pitiful

[4] *Sir Thomas More,* II. 4.

Elizabethan view of the monarch who, in Daniel's noble lines—

Environed with deceit, hemmed in with guile,
Soothed up in flattery, fawned on of all,
Within his own living as in exile,
Hears but with others' ears or not at all.[5]

Absolutism had come in and with it its characteristic art. "Princes' images on their tombs do not lie as they were wont," says Webster, "seeming to pray up to Heaven, but with their hands under their cheeks, as if they died of the toothache." [6] *Othello* and *Lear* are Baroque tragedies as *Measure for Measure* and *Cymbeline* are Baroque comedies. They have all the characteristics of Baroque art: the sensationalism, the extravagant emotional attitudes, "as if they had died of the toothache"; the sentimentality, particularly in the portraits of women; even the desire to shock. Shakespeare leads the fashion rather than follows it, for the "romances" do not begin with *Philaster* or *Pericles* but with *Othello* and *Lear*. Evade the physical catastrophe of *Lear* and you have a Baroque comedy; add the final catastrophe to *A Winter's Tale* and you have a Baroque tragedy.

But one cannot place the responsibility entirely on any form of art, however fashionable it may have been. That must rest on Shakespeare himself and the blind tyrannous strength which would not be satisfied with anything but inhuman abstractions like Iago and Edmund as the instruments of destiny, and which uses

[5] *Civil Wars.*

[6] *The Duchess of Malfi,* IV. 2.

them in an overmastering impulse to crush and destroy, even to the very seed in the womb.

Chapter 11

The Bad Texts

THE COMMENTATORS suggest that there is a lightening of the misanthropic gloom in *Macbeth* and *Antony and Cleopatra,* but this is merely the rounding off of a sentimental romance composed by themselves of which the hero is not Shakespeare but Beethoven. If these two plays are outstanding among the tragedies it is because they are histories, and since Shakespeare had merely to tell a familiar story over again, he could not wreak his misanthropy on them.

In them the nervous disintegration of language that was hinted at in earlier plays becomes marked. *Hamlet* and *Troilus and Cressida,* apart from their classicisms and Gallicisms, contain a number of grammatical perversions; nouns are used as verbs, adjectives as nouns, and so forth: a verb like "to business" in *Hamlet* is typical. Again, *Hamlet* contains the lines "No, let the candied tongue, lick absurd pomp, and crook the pregnant hinges of the knee." Because these read peculiarly all editors carefully correct them to "No, let the candied tongue lick absurd pomp, and crook the pregnant hinges of the knee" which is insane. Shakespeare punctuated the passage quite correctly because he intended "candied" as a noun and "tongue" as a verb.

In *King Lear* we get rather more of it: verbs like

"stranger," "monster," "worthy," "hovel," and "knee," and adjectives like "looped," "windowed," and "husbanded." In *Antony and Cleopatra* it becomes a landslide: verbs like "ballad," "boy," "antick," "spaniel," "lackey," "boot," "bark," "safe," and "demure"; as well as the even more characteristic nouns in "er" like "sworder," "master-leaver," "hater," "equaliser," "feeder," and "homager," particularly in harsh compounds like "putter-out." There is a fondness for the verbal noun because of its ambiguity, and so we get "seeming" for "appearance," "becomings" for "charms," "having" for "possessions," and "containing" for "contents," while the verbal noun does double service as an adjective as in "not-fearing Britain" and "rebelling coasts." Transitive verbs become intransitive and the other way round, while on the analogy of "honour" ("the honours were even") abstract nouns are given plural forms as in "shames" and "decays."

In meter there is an even greater disintegration, the midline stop of *Hamlet* giving place to a full close in the middle of a line, sometimes produced by a harsh combination of assonance and alliteration, sometimes by a powerful heaping up of qualified nouns.

Her brother's ghost his pavèd bed would break
And take her hence in horror.[1]

In *Antony and Cleopatra* there is even a looseness of meter like that of Fletcher with his abuse of the feminine ending, that is, the ending of the line with a

[1] *M. for M.*, V. 1.

word of two syllables. The trouble with this is that by infection the feminine ending spreads to the middle of the line, and when the two disyllables move together, as they often do in Fletcher, the five-beat measure of blank verse breaks down and we get one of four beats that jogs happily on like an old pony. Shakespeare's ear was too sensitive to make this mistake often, and when he collaborates with Fletcher a simple glance at the line endings is usually sufficient to tell us who the author is, but still he does make it in *Cymbeline* and *Antony and Cleopatra.*

In a group of plays written somewhere about 1605—*Macbeth,* certain scenes from *Measure for Measure,* and odd speeches in that extraordinary medley of authors and styles *All's Well That Ends Well*—Shakespeare's dramatic style was at it greatest. Experiment in these has gone as far as it can go without injuring the texture of the verse. In *Macbeth* particularly the peculiar mood of exaltation is expressed in the fondness for the word "great" used for color rather than for sense—"the great Doom's image," "in the great hand of God," "our great quell."

Macbeth is a tragedy not of crime but of ambition. An ambitious man himself, Shakespeare was haunted by the idea of power; its seizure by Macbeth, its abuse by Angelo, its achievement by More.

Good God! Good God!
That I from such an humble bench of birth
Should step as 'twere up to my country's head,
And give the law out there! [2]

[2] *Sir Thomas More, Addition III.*

Macbeth himself is not so much a good man gone wrong as an ambitious one who has discovered the mockery of power. Death, the ultimate horror, he has inflicted on Duncan, but Duncan in his grave has the peace Macbeth has lost: "steel nor poison, malice domestic, foreign levy, nothing can touch him further." This is no longer the death which to the young Shakespeare had seemed almost as natural as life; it is the death of the oversensitive man, the death of the suicide, the only panacea for the horrors of life. "Fear no more the frown of the great, thou art past the tyrant's stroke." The same misanthropy appears in the repetition of the theme of the broken seed pod:

> *though the treasure*
> *Of Nature's germens tumble all together*
> *Even till Destruction sicken.*[3]

Unfortunately, these three plays have come down to us in abominable texts, and we can only guess at what the original plays were like. For instance, on April 20, 1611, a quack doctor and astrologer named Simon Forman saw *Macbeth* at the Globe Theatre and later wrote a fairly full account of it. "Macbeth and Banquo, two noblemen of Scotland, riding through a wood, there stood before them three women fairies or nymphs." Later, "When Macbeth had murdered the King, the blood on his hands would not be washed off by any means, nor from his wife's hands, which handled the bloody daggers in hiding them."

The play itself was not printed until the Folio of 1623 and in this, our only text, occur two concerted

[3] *Macb.*, IV. 1.

numbers, mentioned only by name, which also occur in Middleton's *The Witch*. Since they contain references to characters in Middleton's play they clearly belong to it, not to *Macbeth,* and as they require the presence of Hecate it is plain that they are the sole reason for her appearance in Shakespeare's play. Accordingly, it is generally agreed that the Hecate speech and the concerted numbers are interpolations and that they were introduced by Thomas Middleton himself; that he also tampered with the second scene and that he or someone else cut the play.

I am not satisfied with this conclusion because it seems to me to ignore the principal difficulty: the Holinshed print of the three respectable ladies, the passage in Holinshed that describes how Macbeth and Banquo, "passing through the *woods* and fields," came upon three women, "either the weird sisters, that is (as ye would say) the goddesses of destiny, or else some nymphs or fairies," and Simon Forman's description of the performance of *Macbeth* he saw in which Macbeth and Banquo, "riding through a wood," saw "three women fairies or nymphs." What one wants to know is how the three woodland nymphs became translated into the three witches of the blasted heath in the Stewpan scenes. This is important because the sort of *Macbeth* Forman describes would be suitable for an open-air theater like the Globe while the Stewpan episodes would be highly impracticable in any but an indoor one.

Again, Forman, an astrologer as well as a quack, never refers to the apparitions scene. Is this not because there was no such scene in the original *Macbeth,* since it would have been difficult and ineffective on an open-air stage? And what on earth has happened to the scene in which Macbeth and his wife tried to wash their hands after the murder? "A little water clears us of this deed," but it does not clear the text of lines like "Will all great Neptune's ocean wash this blood clean from my hand?" and its echoes in Lady Macbeth's sleepwalking.

The text, as I have said, is atrocious: the line "we have scorched the snake not killed it" seems to have been lifted from a scene which took place after the murder of Banquo and to refer to the escape of Fleance rather than to the murder of Duncan. The entrance of the Murderers during the banquet scene (almost impossible to stage) seems to have been dragged in for effect, while it must be obvious to the meanest intelligence that neither Shakespeare nor Burbadge could be responsible for the off-stage death of the principal character and the appearance of his head on a pole. Clearly, this is the work of a stage director. The stage director *had* a head and needed a part for it.

The text is as corrupt as *Measure for Measure*. Poor school children are compelled to work their way through lines like the following though no scholar I know of even dares to suggest what they mean.

> *If th' asssassination*
> *Could trammel up the consequence and catch*
> *With this surcease, success;* that but *this blow*
> *Might* be *the* be-*all and the end-all,* here
> But here *upon this* bank and shoal *of time*
> *We'd jump the life to come.*[4]

[4] *Macb.,* I. 7.

"Be-all" and "end-all," though sanctified by generations of hardworking journalists, look very like ghost words; "here but here" is plain nonsense; "bank and shoal"—Theobald's emendation of "Banke and schoole"—is a scholar's idea of poetry. As the image appears to be from a court of oyer and terminer, one can only surmise that Shakespeare wrote something like:

Might be the trial and the endal, heard
*But here upon this bank and stool of time.**

It seems to me that editors have ignored the most flagrant signs of revision. One scene opens like this:

LADY M.: Is Banquo gone from court?
SERV.: Ay, madam, but returns again tonight.
LADY M.: Say to the King I would attend his leisure
For a few words.
SERV.: Madam, I will. (*Exit* SERVANT.)
LADY M.: Nought's had all's spent
Where our desire is got without content:
'Tis safer to be that which we destroy
Than by destruction dwell in doubtful joy.
(*Enter* MACBETH.)[5]

There are some remarkable things about this passage. One is the extraordinary clumsiness of the preparation for Macbeth's entrance; the Servant has been introduced merely to summon him, and the couplets to

* At the risk of adding another ghost word to the canon, I would suggest that "be-all" should be "abeyal" for "abeyance," meaning "the contemplation of law."
[5] *Macb.*, III. 2.

fill the gap while Lady Macbeth "attends his leisure." As I shall show, this particular weakness is not confined to *Macbeth.* Another remarkable thing is that the couplets occur in a vastly superior blank verse form in Macbeth's first speech after his entrance.

Better be with the dead
Whom we to gain our peace have sent to peace
Than on the torture of the mind to lie
In restless ecstasy.[6]

At first sight it would seem as if some reviser had translated Shakespeare's blank verse into rhymed couplets to fill a gap in a scene of his own. But is this what did happen? Is the rhyme betweeen "lie" and "ecstasy" a mere accident? *All's Well That Ends Well,* at least so far as the verse goes, must be almost contemporary with *Macbeth.* It is a play about a poor girl who, having got herself married to a nobleman, tricks him into consummating the marriage by acting as substitute for an Italian girl he is in love with. As in *Macbeth* there is a lot of dull rhymed verse, but the peculiar feature of this is that it seems to be Shakespeare who translates the rhymed couplets into blank verse, transforming them by a few strokes into magnificent poetry.

But O strange men!
That can such sweeet use make of what they hate
When saucy trusting of the cozened thoughts
Defiles the pitchy night: so lust doth play
With what it loathes for that which is away.[7]

6 *Macb.,* III. 2.
7 *A. W. E. W.,* IV. 4.

Or this, with its characteristic repetition of the "Ne'er loved till lost" theme that haunted him.

Love that comes too late
Like a remorseful pardon slowly carried
To the great sender turns a sour offence
Crying 'That's good that's gone.' Our rash faults
Make trivial price of serious things we have
Not knowing them until we know their graves:
Oft our displeasures to ourselves unjust
Destroy our friends and after weep their dust.[8]

The translation has been so swiftly done that Shakespeare sometimes leaves the rhymes sticking out like fossils in his text.

that can'st not dream
We poising us in her defective scale,
Can weigh thee to the beam; *that wilt not* know
It is in us to plant thine honour where
We please to have it grow.[9]

The scene from which the latter passage is taken is an extraordinary bit of work. It opens with Bertram, Lafeu, and Parolles discussing Helena's restoration of the King to health, though Bertram's sole contribution to the discussion is "And so 'tis." The King and Helena appear, accompanied by courtiers and taking no notice of Lafeu and Parolles, while Bertram, with no leave-taking, is presently discovered among the wards whom the King summons so that Helena may choose herself a husband. When she has done this, Lafeu and Parol-

[8] *A. W. E. W.*, V. 3.
[9] *A. W. E. W.*, II. 3.

les "stay behind, commenting of this wedding," as a curious stage direction informs us. It seems clear that Bertram's presence at the opening of the scene is an error, that his real entrance is with the other wards, and that the scene in verse has been spatchcocked into a prose scene between Lafeu and Parolles. Furthermore, the author of the prose scene, who has worked over the verse and given an occasional line to Lafeu to link him with the action, must be Shakespeare. The "dictionary" line he gives Lafeu—"In a most weak and debile minister"—is typically Shakespearean. So is the verse when it is released from its strait jacket of rhyme.

KING: Fair maid, send forth thine eye: this youthful parcel
Of noble bachelors stand at my bestowing,
O'er whom both sovereign power and father's voice
I have to *use:* thy frank election make;
Thou'st power to *choose* and they none to forsake.
HEL.: To each of you one fair and virtuous mistress
Fall when love please! marry, to each but one!
LAF.: I'd give bay Curtal and his furniture
My mouth were no more broken than these boys'
And writ as little beard.
KING: Peruse them well
Not one of these but had a noble father.
HEL.: Gentlemen,
Heaven hath through me restored the king to *health.*
ALL: We understand it and thank Heaven for you.
HEL.: I am a simple maid and therein *wealthiest*
That I protest I simply am a maid.
Please it your majesty, I have done already:

The blushes in my cheeks thus whisper me,
'We blush that thou should'st *choose*; but be *refused*
Let the white death sit on thy cheek forever;
We'll ne'er come there again.'

KING: Make choice; and see
Who shuns thy love shuns all his love in me.[10]

No one can doubt that this is a scene in rhymed verse that has been hastily revised, or doubt that the reviser of it was Shakespeare. It contains some fine verse, but the couplets stick up through it, not only in the obvious rhymes but also in the suppressed ones like "parcel (band)—stand" and "election (choice)—voice."

But somebody else must have been at work on it, because at the end of the verse scene we get the note that "Parolles and Lafeu stay behind commenting of this wedding," which, as Professor Wilson has pointed out, is not a stage direction at all and can only be explained as an instruction to a collaborator. He takes the view that it is Shakespeare who is giving the instruction, but if Shakespeare wrote the scene between Lafeu and Parolles why should he give instructions to himself?

One might, of course, assume that the rhymed verse comes from the early play, *Love's Labour's Won,* of which *All's Well* is generally supposed to be a revision. There is certainly one speech that comes from a Shakespeare play of the early 1590's and indubitably links it with the Marriage sonnets. That is the tirade on Virginity—"Out with it! within ten year it will make

[10] *A. W. E. W.*, II. 3.

itself ten, which is a goodly increase, and the principal itself not much the worse: away with it!" But this, too, has been tampered with, for at this point Helena is made to ask: "How might one do, sir, to lose it to her own liking?" and Parolles replies, "Let me see: marry, ill to like him that ne'er it likes." After which piece of fatuity, the tirade swings on as before. And how, if Shakespeare really was the author of the rhymed verse, did he come to make the mistake he makes in this scene? It continues in this way:

HEL.: Now, Dian, from thy altar do I fly,
And to imperial Love, that god most high,
Do my sighs stream. Sir, will you hear my suit?
1ST LORD: And grant it.
HEL.: Thanks, sir; all the rest is mute.
LAF.: I had rather be in this choice than throw ames ace for my life.
HEL.: The honour, sir, that flames in your fair eyes
Before I speak too threateningly replies:
Love make your fortune twenty times above
Her that so wishes and her humble love.
2ND LORD: No better, if you please.
HEL.: My wish receive,
Which great Love grant! and so I take my leave.
LAF.: Do all they deny her? An' they were sons of mine I'd have them whipped; or I would send them to the Turk to be made eunuchs of.
HEL.: Be not afraid I your hand should take;
I'll never do you wrong for your own sake:
Blessings upon your vows, and in your bed
Find fairer fortune if you ever wed.
LAF.: These boys are boys of ice, they'll none have

her: sure they are bastards to the English; the French ne'er got 'em.[11]

Now, as Professor Wilson points out, the meaning of this is that all the lads except Bertram are eager to marry Helena, and Helena, like the great lady she is, lets them down lightly by affecting to think that they are alarmed at the prospect—an admirable piece of comedy if the author had taken the trouble to write it. But the curious thing is that Lafeu also believes that none of them wants to marry Helena. Professor Wilson puts him and Parolles "at a distance," but I cannot imagine any stage distance that would make this point clear to an audience. Just think of the difficulties the producer faces! He must make it plain that each of the young lords is eager to be chosen as Helena's partner though none of them has a line that makes this unequivocally clear; that Helena doesn't want to marry any of them, at the same time expressing her belief that none of them wants to marry her, and that Lafeu, acting as chorus and completely misinterpreting the whole scene, is just making a mistake. Without testing it in rehearsal, I should say it would result in chaos. Surely what has happened is that in his careless revision of the scene he has been partially revising, Shakespeare has made the same mistake Professor Wilson accuses Lafeu of making.

[11] *A. W. E. W.*, II. 3.

Chapter 12

Measure for Measure

IT IS ONLY WITH *Measure for Measure* that we get sufficient material for textual criticism. The New Cambridge editor, Professor Wilson, has produced a most brilliant analysis of the text, but the conclusions he draws from it are disappointing. They are that the play was abridged for Court performance on December 26, 1604, and some time after November, 1606, expanded again into prose, Shakespeare not being consulted in either operation. He credits Shakespeare with 1,865 lines; "of these 1,604 are in blank verse, and no one we think will be inclined to doubt that all this, whether its style be early or late, is from Shakespeare's hand." The rest of the play is the "reviser's."

The story is roughly this: the Duke of Vienna retires to a monastery, leaving the government of the city in the hands of the puritanical Angelo, who re-enacts the laws against fornication, and condemns Claudio to death. Claudio's sister, Isabella, a novice in a convent, pleads for him, and Angelo offers to reprieve him if she becomes his mistress. The Duke, now acting as chaplain of the prison, overhears her telling this to Claudio, and persuades her to allow a lady jilted by Angelo, one "Mariana of the Moated Grange," to keep the tryst instead of her. Angelo, believing he has possessed Isabella and afraid of her brother's vengeance, orders Claudio's execution. The Duke has the head of another prisoner sent to him instead, and then stages a showdown in which Isabella accuses Angelo, who gives her the lie; Mariana of the Moated Grange denies Isabella's charges and claims Angelo for herself, only to be repudiated in her turn (all, scene for scene, very much in the manner of *All's Well That Ends Well*), till finally the Duke himself, returning in his monk's habit, makes a fresh charge before revealing his identity, resurrecting Claudio, and proposing to Isabella.

There is nothing wrong with the main theme. It might have made a magnificent tragedy in the manner of *Othello;* a fine study of a weak man in the manner of *Promos and Cassandra,* on which it is based, or a satiric comedy like *Tartufe.* All these possibilities were barred, because onto the original powerful tale was grafted the fanciful theme of *All's Well That Ends Well,* and the introduction of Mariana of the Moated Grange made it necessary that Angelo should be pardoned and therefore robbed the play of all dramatic impulse. It is not that there is anything inherently wrong with the theme of *All's Well That Ends Well.* If one assumes that it is a reworking of *Love's Labour's Won* and was originally written at the same time as the Marriage sonnets, one can see that Shakespeare, whose patron, the Earl of Southampton, was at the time kicking against his proposed marriage to the granddaughter of the Secretary, Lord Burghley, could have got considerable fun out of the subject of a ward of the court who refuses to marry the commoner that the King has chosen as his wife, and who is finally outwitted by her. But no total conception of a play can combine in one moral perception the theme of a governor who forces a pious girl into his bed and that of a clever girl who tricks a wayward man into hers. *Measure for Measure* is not one play but two, and the two do not blend; they do not even collide with one another; they merely meet and back away.

The problem is how did Shakespeare ever come to write such a play? In fact, did he really write such a play, or is there, behind *Measure for Measure,* an entirely different sort of play? That revision or collaboration took place there is no doubt at all. The evidence for this is of a different kind from that in *All's Well That Ends Well.* There are rhymed couplets in *Measure for Measure* and some of them are clearly not Shakespeare's, but there is far more impressive evidence than this. In III. 1. there is a change from verse to prose of which the New Cambridge editors write with commendable restraint that "the two halves of this scene cannot be made of a piece by anyone possessing even a rudimentary acquaintance with English prose and poetry. We will not say they could not have been written—an interval granted—by the same man. But we say confidently that they could not have been written by the same man at one spell, on one inspiration, or with anything like an identical or even continuous poetic purpose." To this the editor of the Temple Shakespeare replies by saying that "Shakespeare wrote the scene with a deliberately *dis*continuous *dramatic* purpose"—whatever that may mean.

Shakespeare did not write the scene at all, at any time, and the evidence is not in the difference of style—though heaven knows that is obvious enough for anyone; it is in two passages that I must quote in full. The act opens in the prison with the Duke (disguised as a friar), Claudio, and the Provost. (We shall see later what the Provost is doing here.) The Duke comforts Claudio in the great speech on death, and then Isabella's voice is heard outside.

ISAB.: What ho! Peace here; grace and good company!
PROV.: Who's there? come in: the wish deserves a welcome.
DUKE: Dear sir, ere long I'll visit you again.
CLAUD.: Most holy sir, I thank you. (*Enter* ISABELLA.)
ISAB.: My business is a word or two with Claudio.
PROV.: And very welcome. Look, signior, here's your sister.
DUKE: Provost, a word with you.
PROV.: As many as you please.
DUKE: Bring me to hear them speak where I may be concealed. (*Exeunt* DUKE *and* PROVOST.)[1]

Now, this is a remarkable passage in itself; a fussy, confused, and undramatic passage, but nothing like so bad as one that occurs later. In one of the greatest scenes in literature Isabella tells Claudio of Angelo's proposal; he breaks down and begs her to accept it, and she pours scorn on him. Her speech is interrupted by the sudden emergence of the Duke from hiding, and it is of this joint between verse and prose that the New Cambridge editors say that "the two halves of this scene cannot be made of a piece by anyone possessing even a rudimentary acquaintance with English prose and poetry." It is curious that they fail to notice that the style of this scene is identical with that of the brief passage I have quoted.

[1] *M. for M.*, III. 1.

DUKE: Vouchsafe a word, young sister, but one word.
ISAB.: What is your will?
DUKE: Might you dispense with your leisure, I would by and by have some speech with you: *the satisfaction I would require is likewise your own benefit.*
ISAB.: I have no superfluous leisure; my stay must be stolen out of other affairs; but I will attend you awhile. (*Walks apart.*)
DUKE: Son, I have overheard what hath passed between you and your sister. Angelo had never the purpose to corrupt her; only he hath made an assay of her virtue to practice his judgment with the disposition of natures; she, having the truth of honour in her, hath made him that gracious denial which he is most glad to receive. I am confessor to Angelo, and I know this to be true; therefore prepare yourself to death; do not satisfy your resolution with hopes that are fallible; tomorrow you must die; go to your knees and make ready.
CLAUD.: Let me ask my sister pardon. I am so out of love with life that I will sue to be rid of it.
DUKE: Hold you there: farewell. (*Exit* CLAUDIO.) Provost, a word with you! (*Re-enter* PROVOST.)
PROV.: What's your will, father?
DUKE: That now you are come you will be gone. Leave me awhile with the maid: my mind promises with my habit no loss shall touch her by my company.
PROV.: In good time.[2]

The curious points about this passage are numerous. First, there is the phrase I have italicized and to which I shall return. Second, there is the fact that the Duke is

[2] *M. for M.*, III. 1.

not only masquerading as a friar, but even hearing confessions and ostensibly revealing the substance of them, a piece of Protestant legend that would come ill from the friend of Strange and Southampton. Third, there is the deliberate and cruel lying of the Duke; fourth, the fact that Claudio, having asked leave to beg his sister's pardon, goes out without saying a word to her. But all these become unimportant beside the one glaring fact that the author has not the remotest idea of how to get people on and off the stage. He has had to get Isabella to "walk apart" while the Duke tells her brother lies; he has had to get Claudio out of the condemned cell unaccompanied by any gaoler so that the Duke can talk to Isabella: worst of all, he has had to withdraw the Provost from their common hiding place and dismiss him. Beyond question, this is the writing of a man who did not know the theater.

But why has he tied himself up into this extraordinary knot? The explanation is, I think, fairly clear. Neither the Duke nor the Provost has any business on the stage at all. In Shakespeare's version of the scene Claudio and Isabella fought their battle to a conclusion, whatever that was. Then the Duke met Isabella coming from her brother's cell, and learned her story. Presumably she was accompanied by the Provost because "no loss shall touch her by my company" is good Shakespeare. At first the Duke was incredulous; we get a brief fragment of his part irrelevantly intruded upon a later scene.

his life is paralleled
Even with the stroke and line of his great justice:
He doth with holy abstinence subdue
That in himself which he spurs on his power

To qualify in others: were he mealed with that
Which he corrects, then were he tyrannous;
But this being so he's just.[3]

When the Duke realized the truth of what Isabella was saying, there was the Shakespearean peripateia. Alas, that scene exists only in a murdered form in the reviser's prose, but we can still get some small idea of what it was like.

The hand that hath made you fair hath made you good:
The goodness that is cheap in beauty makes
(Its) beauty brief in goodness, but (His) grace,
Being the soul of your complexion,
Shall keep the body of it ever fair.[4]

Not wishing to repeat the scene between Claudio and Isabella, the hack intruded the Duke and Provost upon it. That is why I remarked upon the presence of the Provost at the opening of the scene. He must be there to show the Duke a hiding place, and when the Duke leaves it, and Claudio, who he is supposed to be guarding, has wandered off, he must be summoned and dismissed in the most ridiculous lines in dramatic literature. "What's your will, father?" "That now you are come you will be gone." Here one can go considerably further than the New Cambridge editor and say that no one possessing a rudimentary acquaintance with the theater can possibly suppose that this is the work of a dramatist.

[3] *M. for M.*, IV. 2.
[4] *M. for M.*, III. 1.

But what is he? Professor Wilson believes he is the man who revised and expanded the play at some time after November, 1606, but in this scene we have positive proof that he was not expanding but telescoping, in the manner of the man who seems to have telescoped two different scenes in *The Two Gentlemen of Verona*. The problem we have to ask ourselves now is, why was he telescoping? To cut the repetition of Isabella's complaint, undoubtedly, but there must have been a further reason. If the plot had developed as we now have it; if Angelo was to have been fobbed off with Mariana of the Moated Grange instead of Isabella, there would have been no reason why, once having established his cut, the "reviser" should not have allowed the plot to be revealed in Shakespeare's own words instead of going to all the trouble of composing his own dreary speeches, such as "This forenamed maid hath yet in her the continuance of her first affection: his unjust kindness, that in all reason should have quenched her love, hath, like an impediment in the current, made it more violent and unruly." [5]

The reason why the reviser could not make use of Shakespeare's speeches was that Shakespeare never wrote them. Shakespeare never conceived of the existence of Mariana of the Moated Grange, even if she was a character in his scenario. The whole point of the tremendous tragedy that Shakespeare was writing was that Angelo had had no experience of women. The Angelo he imagined was a saint, and his tragedy was that he could be tempted only by a saint. That is the meaning of his terrible cry—

[5] *M. for M.*, III. 1.

O cunning Enemy, that, to catch a saint,
With saints dost bait thy hook! Most dangerous
Is that temptation that doth goad us on
To sin in loving virtue. . . .[6]

Whether as I most often think, Shakespeare had written a play called *Measure for Measure,* of which our present text is merely a parody, or whether he had collaborated at a distance with a man who was completely incapable of fulfilling his intentions, there is no doubt in my mind that Mariana of the Moated Grange had no real place in it.

So long as the scenario follows the original one of *Promos and Cassandra* there is no problem. The first part of the play is masterly. The scenes between Angelo and Isabella and the scene between Isabella and Claudio are for me among the greatest things in Shakespearean drama. Criticism of Isabella and Angelo is usually fatuous, because commentators fail to realize that both are saints and their standards are not ours. The indictment is not of piety but of power, Acton's belief that absolute power corrupts absolutely. But the reviser, or collaborator, was obsessed by the theme of *All's Well That Ends Well* and could not see that the introduction of Mariana of the Moated Grange would inevitably result in a reconciliation scene that would call off the dogs of drama; and from the moment the lady's name is mentioned the play goes to pieces. All the prose of the prison scene in which we are told her sad story is the hack's. Need we ask who was the author of the scene in which we meet her first? This scene, which editors love to place confi-

[6] *M. for M.*, II. 2.

dently at "the Moated Grange at St. Luke's," begins with the heavenly "Take O take those lips away" and the singer is dismissed as the Duke enters to a volley of rhymed couplets.

MAR.: Let me excuse me, and believe me so,
  My mirth it much displeased, but pleased my woe.
DUKE: 'Tis good; though music oft hath such a charm
  To make bad good, and good provoke to harm.
  I pray you, tell me, hath any body inquired for me here to-day? much upon this time have I promised here to meet.
MAR.: You have not been inquired after; I have sat here all day. (*Enter* ISABELLA.)
DUKE: I do constantly believe you. The time is come even now. I shall crave your forbearance a little: may be I will call upon you anon, *for some advantage to yourself.*
MAR.: I am always bound to you. (*Exit* MARIANA.) [7]

The first thing that needs to be pointed out to all editors of *Measure for Measure* is that in this extraordinary scene not one word indicates who the strange lady is, or for what purpose the Duke has visited her. The fact that they deal so much in stage directions and speech entries blinds them to the fact that these are not visible to an audience. Anyhow, Mariana's exit at this point is the low-water mark of dramatic incompetence.

But surely we have met before this man who finds such inordinate difficulty in exits and entrances and tries to cover up the huggermugger in which he involves himself by making his characters say myste-

[7] *M. for M.*, IV. 1.

riously "*It shall be for your good.*" Here he comes again, now that Isabella has explained the details of her arrangement for meeting Angelo.

DUKE: 'Tis well borne up.
I have not yet made known to Mariana
A word of this. What ho! within! come forth!
(*Re-enter* MARIANA.)
I pray you, be acquainted with this maid;
She comes to do you good.
ISAB.: I do desire the like.
DUKE: Do you persuade yourself that I respect you?
MAR.: Good friar, I know you do, and have found it.
DUKE: Take then, this your companion by the hand,
Who hath a story ready for your ear.
I shall attend your leisure: but make haste;
The vaporous night approaches.
MAR.: Will't please you walk aside? (*Exeunt* MARIANA *and* ISABELLA.)
DUKE: O place and greatness! millions of false eyes
Are stuck upon thee; volumes of report
Run with these false and most contrarious quests
Upon thy doings: thousand scapes of wit
Make thee the father of their idle dreams
And rack thee in their fancies. (*Re-enter* MARIANA *and* ISABELLA.) Welcome! How agreed?
ISAB.: She'll take the enterprise upon her, father,
If you advise it.[8]

Now every Shakespearean student has noticed one thing about this scene: that the speech on place and

[8] *M. for M.*, IV. 1.

greatness does not belong here; it belongs in III. 2., where Lucio traduces the Duke to the supposed Friar and the Duke says:

> *No might or greatness in mortality*
> *Can censure scape; back-wounding calumny*
> *The whitest virtue strikes. What king so strong*
> *Can tie the gall up in the slanderous tongue?* [9]

Professor Wilson believes that the two passages are continuous and have been chopped up in this way because the reviser wished to cover up a cut. Sir Edmund Chambers believes that they are not continuous and I feel sure he is right because I don't for an instant believe that the couplets are Shakespeare's. Remember that we have already met with precisely the same thing in *Macbeth,* even to the similarity of phrasing between "I would attend his leisure" and "I shall attend your leisure," only that in *Macbeth* the reviser used his own couplets to plug up a hole in the scene, while here he uses Shakespeare's blank verse. Why? To cover up a cut, replies Professor Wilson. But is this the only reason?

It is true that, if, as I have suggested, the machinery of Angelo's downfall was differently planned by Shakespeare, there must at this point have been drastic cutting. To judge by the way the scene is written here, it seems unlikely that Isabella and her substitute met at all. The Duke must have taken the whole contrivance upon himself, learning the details of the tryst from Isabella and repeating them to

[9] *M. for M.*, III. 2.

Isabella's substitute. But for me the most important thing about the scene is that here again we have our old friend who "comes to do us good" and finds such difficulty about getting in and out to do it; and that the reason he has used Shakespeare's lines as a stopgap is that he has tied himself into one of his usual knots. We must remember that we are seeing Mariana for the first time and that she is seeing Isabella for the first time, and that some sort of exposition scene is necessary. The time for this is immediately after Isabella's entrance, but as Isabella has to reveal the arrangements for her tryst with Angelo, which in the original must have been an independent scene that probably took place at Isabella's convent, and the reviser has no notion of how to weld the two scenes together, he gets Mariana off-stage with his usual promise of an improvement in her fortunes. But now, after Isabella has spoken, he is in a worse plight than ever, for the Duke or Isabella must now explain it all over again to Mariana, with the addition of her own proposed part in the tryst; and as this is entirely beyond his powers, he cuts the Gordian knot by letting his ladies "walk apart" while he uses six lines of Shakespeare quite irrelevantly to fill up the interval of forty seconds in which Isabella may be supposed to tell the other woman the story of her life.

Once more, we can put our finger on this scene and say that it must be obvious to anyone who has the remotest acquaintance with the theater that it was not written by a dramatist. With these clues to the capacity of the hack we can easily test other scenes for his presence. Here is one scene where it is very obvious. It is just before Angelo sends the order for Claudio's execution.

DUKE: The best and wholesomest spirits of the night
Envelop you, good Provost! Who called here of late?

PROV.: None since the curfew rung.

DUKE: Not Isabel?

PROV.: No.

DUKE: They will then ere't be long.

PROV.: What comfort is for Claudio?

DUKE: There's some in hope.

PROV.: It is a bitter deputy.

DUKE: Not so, not so; his life is paralleled
Even with the stroke and line of his great justice:
He doth with holy abstinence subdue
That in himself which he spurs on his power
To qualify in others: were he mealed with that
Which he corrects, then were he tyrannous;
But this being so he's just. (*Knocking within.*)
Now are they come.
(*aside*) This is a gentle provost: seldom when
The steeled gaoler is the friend of men. (*Knocking within.*)
How now! What noise? That spirit's possessed with haste
That wounds the unsisting postern with these strokes.

PROV. There he must stay until the officer
Arise to let him in: he is called up.

DUKE: Have you no countermand for Claudio yet? [10]

Here once more we have an entrance handled with childlike incompetence. It is made still more incompetent by editors who give the Provost an exit and

[10] *M. for M.*, IV. 2.

immediate re-entrance when the knocking is heard. As in the scene at the Moated Grange we have the Duke asking whether someone hasn't inquired for him and when told that no one has, giving assurance that somebody soon will. Again we have a speech—"his life is paralleled"—of pure Shakespearean texture, even to the diction line. "Even with the stroke and line of his great justice" in a context where it is dramatically meaningless, since the Duke already knows that Angelo's "holy abstinence" no longer exists; and once more we can say confidently that the speech has been taken from its real context, which was either the scene between the Duke and Isabella in which the Duke learned for the first time of Angelo's backsliding or that between the Duke and Lucio in III.2. placed here with grotesque clumsiness to lengthen the interval between two successive entrances. If any reader has followed me so far he will probably agree either that Shakespeare was writing "with a deliberately *dis*-continuous *dramatic* purpose" or that Professor Wilson's view that "no one . . . will be inclined to doubt that all this, whether its style be early or late, is from Shakespeare's hand" is overoptimistic.

By this time the tragical and farcical themes have become so hopelessly confused that it is difficult to see exactly what purpose the hack had in writing this particular scene at all. Judging by the previous two scenes where we can detect his hand, I would guess that the Duke was not supposed to be in the prison. It seems to me probable that Angelo's order for Claudio's execution did not demand the production of Claudio's head at all, but that the hack wanted a head brought on stage. He certainly revised the last act of

Macbeth with no other purpose than to have Macbeth's head brought on, probably believing it to be highly dramatic. The bloodthirsty tomfoolery in which the Duke (supposedly a mere chaplain) orders the execution of Barnardine, and then, when Barnardine refuses to make his confession to the Duke, relents and has the head of a dead prisoner cut off instead, contains a solecism that would have irritated an Elizabethan audience more than it irritates us. Pompey, now a hangman's apprentice, summons Barnardine to be hanged, but the hangman asks "Is the axe upon the block, sirrah?" To an Elizabethan this would have been absurd. Beheading would have been the fate of a nobleman like Claudio, hanging the fate of a common thief like Barnardine. There is something dreadfully out of key about these scenes, and I cannot help wondering if Shakespeare did not intend that Claudio should be saved from the block *not* by the Duke but by the friendly Provost, and if Claudio's appearance in the last scene was not intended to be as much a surprise to the Duke as to everyone else. It is very suspicious that the Duke's later speeches all imply his belief in Claudio's death, and it is really too much to ask us to accept them as a gentle leg-pulling of Isabella. It is still more suspicious that, when Claudio is finally produced, he has not a single word to say for himself.

I am afraid this is as far as criticism of the text can go. There is no doubt that, early or late, there was a complete *Measure for Measure* in Shakespeare's hand. I suspect that it was early; I have noted certain similarities between it, "the Rape of Lucrece," and *Edward II*. I have also a strong impression that the glorious scene of Pompey's examination before the magistrates is really early Shakespeare, written not for Armin but for Kempe. The urbanity and detachment of Escalus' advice to Constable Elbow—"because he hath some offences in him that thou would'st discover if thou could'st, let him continue in his courses till thou knowest what they are"—has all the sunny quality of the early plays. But a large part of the play as we have it now, particularly the first two acts, is in Shakespeare's later manner, and we can say of the first two acts at least that even if there had never been a reviser, even if the last three acts had not been metamorphosed into a silly and often disgusting farce, no play built on the scenario that Shakespeare seems to have been using would have stood up to them. They are Shakespeare at his very gravest and most passionate, preoccupied from the first moment with the problem of power, its relation to God and its proneness to evil. This is largely obscured by the editors' perpetuation of the meaningless Jacobean "Heaven" when Shakespeare clearly wrote "God."

> *Which sorrow is always towards ourselves, not* God
> *Showing we would not spare* God *as we love* Him
> *But as we stand in fear.*[11]

So too in the blasphemous bowdlerization of "*God*'s image" and more obviously (since the hack neglected to change the pronoun) in

> God *in my mouth*
> *As if I only did but chew His name.*[12]

[11] *M. for M.*, II. 3.
[12] *M. for M.*, II. 4.

The hack wanted merely a ballet of monks and nuns in the manner of *The Merry Devil of Edmonton,* though that enchanting little play has a wit and grace which the hack could never have understood; his is a slightly salacious and exceedingly sacrilegious masquerade in which the disguised Duke hears everybody's confession and reports the substance of it to anyone willing to listen, and the characters enter to cheerful bursts of "What ho! Peace ho!" It is to be noted that the opening of the scene between Isabella and Lucio in the convent of "the Votarists of St. Clare" is in this style, which is marked by the use of un-Shakespearean words like "manifested," "affianced," and "unsisting" (whatever that may mean), and an extraordinarily stiff use of common words like "constantly" and "combine": "I do *constantly* believe you," "I am *combined* by a sacred vow," and "*combinate* husband."

Whoever the hack was he had the last word, and, as in *Macbeth,* the text of Shakespeare's work is crudely cut and carelessly transcribed. The two great scenes between Isabella and Angelo are in ruin. "We cannot weigh our brother with ourself" should be "You cannot weigh our brother with yourself," and "If not a fedary but only he owe and succeed *thy* weakness" is an obvious error, since not only does Isabella know nothing of Angelo's weakness, but she is speaking in the formal second-person plural and breaks into the contemptuous singular only when she understands the full meaning of his proposal.

Who the hack was is another matter. I have no doubt that the same man worked on *Macbeth,* an impression that he worked also on *The Merry Wives of Windsor, All's Well That Ends Well,* and *Pericles,* and

a suspicion that is little more than a fancy that he als
had something to do with the scenarios of *King Lea*
and *Cymbeline*. There is not sufficient of his work i
any of these to identify him beyond doubt, and simi
larities of vocabulary, such as "manifested," whic
occurs only in the suspect portion of *Merry Wives* an
Measure for Measure, and "vaporous," which occur
only in the Hecate scene of *Macbeth* and the Moate
Grange scene of *Measure for Measure*, are slender. O
the other hand, though it may be only a coincidenc
that the first dreary part of *Pericles* contains a fev
magnificent lines that everyone recognizes as Shake
speare's—"the blind mole casts copped hills toward
heaven, to tell the earth is thronged by man's oppres
sion"—interpolated with utter disregard of their mean
ing, it can scarcely be an accident that again we ge
these cheerful explosions of "Joy and all comfort i
your sacred breast!" "Peace to the lords of Tyre!" an
"Peace be at your labours!" or that the exit of an ob
viously Shakespearean scene should be prepared fo
with "If thou dost hear from me it shall be for th
good." By an extraordinary coincidence we actuall
have external evidence that Shakespeare did not writ
"it shall be for thy good." George Wilkins, the sup
posed collaborator in *Pericles,* who Professor Wilso
believes was also a collaborator in *Measure for Meas
ure,* wrote a novel on the subject after the productio
of the play. Sir Edmund Chambers notes that in a fev
places Wilkins used scraps of blank verse from th
play, but points out that Wilkins also used scraps o
blank verse which are *not* in the play, at least as w
know it. One of these scraps that Sir Edmund isolate
is actually the end of the bawdyhouse scene, and in
stead of "If thou dost hear from me it shall be for th

good" it runs "If you but send to me I am your friend."

It may have been Wilkins who, after Shakespeare's semiretirement from the theater, took on the job of theater poet, and with it the mass production job of adapting popular plays of the Globe Theatre to the indoor theater at Blackfriars. But whatever his function, the man who worked on these plays must also have been a stage director. I can imagine no one else who would have had the last word, as he so clearly had, not only against Shakespeare but against Burbadge. Any tragic actor would have thrown a fit of hysterics at the cutting of his death scene in *Macbeth,* merely to oblige someone who wanted Macbeth's head brought on stage. The last act of *The Merry Wives of Windsor,* the Witches' scenes in *Macbeth,* and a considerable part of *Pericles* look very like the work of someone whose principal task was the production of spectacular effects, and in this he must have had approval from Shakespeare, who would seem to have written in the apparitions scene in *Macbeth* merely to oblige him.

The success that brought Shakespeare's company to the Blackfriars was the beginning of the end for the company and for Shakespeare. The common people who had paid their pennies in the innyards and at the Globe liked poetry; the moneyed upper classes liked dancing and theatrical machinery. Yeats summed it up:

> *Life scarce can cast a fragrance on the wind,*
> *Scarce spread a glory to the morning beams,*
> *But the torn petals strew the garden plot. . . .*

Chapter 13

Antony and Cleopatra

WITH THESE TWO PLAYS, *Macbeth* and *Pericles,* I should feel inclined to agree with Sir Edmund Chambers that Shakespeare suffered a nervous breakdown, and assume that he had been compelled to call in the assistance of a hack, but that they seem to be followed by the perfectly normal *Antony and Cleopatra,* which for me has always been the greatest of the tragedies. In this, as in *Troilus and Cressida,* he has escaped from the limitations of the folk theater. I have no doubt that Shakespeare intended it, like *Coriolanus* and *Timon of Athens,* as satire, because his misanthropy was steadily gaining on him, and the central figure is not so much Antony or Cleopatra as Enobarbus, the mocker. Antony himself is deliberately caricatured in the scene in which he addresses his "sad captains" with the intention of making them weep—the old charmer of *Julius Caesar* having a final fling. But in the process Shakespeare fell in love with Cleopatra himself, and by playing upon the antithesis in himself succeeded in transforming her into a universal figure like Shylock or Falstaff; so that while in *Coriolanus* and *Timon* the storm of misanthropy blows itself out, Cleopatra stands up to it and when she falls, falls like a tower.

She may be drawn from the same model as Cressida; I am inclined to think that Shakespeare imagined an Egyptian proper—a gypsy. Never was there a less queenly queen: she is as common as dirt; she lies, wheedles, deceives, screams, sulks, bites, and makes love with the tireless, un-self-conscious abandonment of an old tinker woman, yet never forfeits our sympathy. If she is not played in this way, as a character part, there is no play. She jokes her way to the highest peaks of tragic poetry, and even an all-merciful God will scarcely forgive an actress who omits to smile at the last "Peace! Peace! Dost thou not see my baby at my breast that sucks the nurse asleep?" Cleopatra is not being acted at all unless the actress hears the magnificent poetry from far away, as though it were being spoken by someone else. Let her try to take advantage of it and illusion vanishes. To herself Cleopatra is simply "a pore girl what's had rotten bad luck with her gentleman friends": it is only to the rest of the world that she is "a lass unparalleled."

In fact, the only rule for any production of *Antony and Cleopatra* is to look after the comedy and let the tragedy look after itself—as it will. Whenever the play fails it is because unconsciously the actors are playing against the lines instead of at once throwing themselves heart and soul into the comedy of the opening scenes. There is no other way to get an audience to accept a tragic heroine who bolts from the battlefield with the gadfly on her, "like a cow in June," [1] and a middle-aged lover who bolts after her "and leaves his navy gazing." [2] Even in phrases like these one can hear the harsh, satiric quality of the verse. Though the romantic in Shakespeare glories in it all, the realist, thinking, as in *Troilus and Cressida* and *Hamlet,* of the absurdity of the reasons for war, keeps reiterating those images of "the three-fold world divided," balancing the

[1] *A. and C.,* III. 9.
[2] *A. and C.,* III. 13.

ecstasies and rages of the middle-aged lovers with the cosmic consequences of their behavior. "Let Rome in Tiber melt and the wide arch of the ranged empire fall"; "so half my Egypt were submerged and made a cistern for scaled snakes"; Antony with "superfluous kings to be his messengers"; Caesar, "the universal landlord," with his army, "the world's great snare," and "a Queen to be his beggar"—never until the last great shriek of "The crown of the world has fallen" does the roar of mockery cease.

It was certainly at this time that Shakespeare began to scribble in the prose revisions of the quarrel scene in *Julius Caesar*. In the original play Brutus and Cassius had quarreled about Cassius' weakness for graft; Shakespeare, rightly considering the motive too abstract for tragedy, revised with the idea of making Brutus hear first of Portia's death. In his later work he had a great fondness for words repeated dully as though the hearer could not quite grasp their full significance or was too full for speech as in Emilia's inert "My husband?" [3] But in the Roman plays the repetition is even duller, like a roll of muffled drums. At its humblest (in *Timon of Athens*) it is:

FIRST LORD. Alcibiades is banished; hear you of it?
FIRST AND SECOND LORD. Alcibiades banished! [4]

In *Coriolanus* it is:

COR.: At Antium lives he?
LAR.: At Antium.[5]

[3] *Oth.*, V. 2.
[4] *Tim.*, III. 6.
[5] *Cor.*, III. 1.

And again:

VOLSCE.: Coriolanus banished!
ROMAN: Banished, sir.[6]

In *Antony and Cleopatra* the echo has been developed until it has a sinister sound which is like distant thunder.
ANT.: Dead then?
MAR.: Dead.[7]

Or—most striking of all:

ANT.: Fulvia is dead.
ENO: Sir?
ANT.: Fulvia is dead.
ENO.: Fulvia?
ANT.: Dead.[8]

The revision of the fourth act of *Julius Caesar* consists mainly of echoes which almost look as though they had merely been scribbled on the margin of the playbook and incorporated by the printer. There is first the false echo of the quarrel scene (I have italicized what I think to be revision).

CAS.: You wrong me every way, you wrong me,
Brutus, I said an elder soldier, not a better.
Did I say better? [9]

6 *Cor.*, IV. 3.
7 *A. and C.*, IV. 14.
8 *A. and C.*, I. 2.
9 *J. C.*, IV. 3.

Immediately on top of this comes a roll of echoes.

CAS.: When Caesar lived he durst not thus have moved me.
BRU.: Peace, peace, you durst not so have tempted him.
CAS.: *I durst not?*
BRU.: *No.*
CAS.: *What? Durst not tempt him?*
BRU.: *For your life you durst not.*

Then the scene draws to a close with an echo of Fulvia's death but more cunningly done.

BRU.: *Portia is dead.*
CAS.: *Ha? Portia?*
BRU.: *She is dead.*
CAS.: *How 'scaped I whipping when I crossed you so?*

After one minor repetition (——*And died so?—— Even so*) the drink goes round. Messala and Titinius arrive and Shakespeare drops his echo, a mere whisper but a marvel of dramatic subtlety—*Portia, art thou gone?* But still the little tune continues to run in his head, and when Brutus makes his report it breaks out again. Notice how it seems to revolve about the idea of death, as though Shakespeare found the wonder of it inexhaustible.

BRU.: Mine speak of seventy senators that died
By their proscription, Cicero being one.
CAS.: *Cicero one?*
MES.: *Cicero is dead.*

For the fanciful, there is plenty of material in Shakespeare's work at this period. In 1609, whoever was responsible, the sonnets were published, and when Coriolanus says "Like a dull actor now I have forgot my part" it is as though he were echoing "the unperfect actor on the stage who with his fear is put beside his part," and when Volumnia cries "for how can we, alas, how can we for our country pray?" it is as though the cadence of "How can it, oh, how can love's eye be true?" were ringing in Shakespeare's head. *Coriolanus,* thanks to the fact that it is history, can only half express Shakespeare's loathing for humanity in the mass, but in *Timon of Athens* all hell breaks loose. It is a curious text, more draft than playbook, with passages in Shakespeare's maturer style oddly intermixed with rhymed verse in the manner of *Macbeth* and the other doubtful plays, but however it came to be written it could never have been successfully produced, for everything in it flows in the same direction. The misanthropy which up to this we have seen only in particular manifestations as hatred of the populace, of sex, and of society, reveals itself as hatred of life. Timon eggs on the whores, "that their activity may defeat and quell the source of all erection"; Nature is told to "ensear her fertile and conceptious womb" that it may "no more bring out ungrateful man"; man is to be utterly destroyed "that beasts may have the world in empire."

There is a similar outburst of misanthropic frenzy in Swift after Stella's death, and at the risk of being fanciful, I cannot help wondering whether the loss of someone who had been dear to him had not left that drum roll in Shakespeare's mind which he heard and reheard in the tone of every voice.

—— Fulvia is dead.
—— Sir?
—— Fulvia is dead.
—— Fulvia?
—— Dead.

Chapter 14

The Baroque Plays

AFTER THAT RATTLE of muffled drums in *Julius Caesar,* Shakespeare's place is with the poets rather than with the dramatists. What the two great masters of the Elizabethan theater had sought was realism of one sort or the other. Shakespeare sought a poetic, humorous realism of which the perfection is to be found in the portraits of Shylock and Falstaff, Dogberry and Pompey Bum; Jonson sought a satiric Renaissance realism such as he achieved in his own gigantic "constructions" which were the *Ulysses* of his own day. Baroque drama cut across both tendencies, for it demanded not realism but expressiveness, and Shakespeare, by drawing upon his own fastidiousness and misanthropy, had made himself the supreme master of Baroque tragedy. Only Beaumont had either the poetic or dramatic gift to approach him in that, but whereas the great scene between Melantius and Calianax in *The Maid's Tragedy* is comparable even with the sleepwalking scene in *Macbeth,* it is naturally Baroque as Shakespeare's is not. Take, for instance, the tapestry scene from the same play, with its ravishing sentimentality, its languorous attitudes, its tremulous repetitions; it is like a piece of Baroque statuary on one of those monuments that John Webster referred to, with real tears carved upon the lovely cheeks.

Do it by me,
Do it again by me, the lost Aspasia,
And you shall find all true but the wild island.
I stand upon the sea-beach now, suppose,
Mine arms thus, and mine hair blown with the wind,
Wild as that desert, and let all about me
Tell that I am forsaken.[1]

Beaumont, with his "take this little prayer" type of sentimentality, is the pure Baroque virtuoso, delighting in the effectiveness of his own situations, whereas Shakespeare can write only out of his own heart, by drawing upon his own experience, and when the storm of misanthropy blows itself out, as it does in *Coriolanus* and *Timon of Athens,* he has exhausted his dramatic capital. Something of the kind had happened to him before, toward the end of the sixteenth century, when his realistic mood, driving him more and more toward observation and away from his personal emotions, was petering out in a sort of brittle comedy. Now, after another ten years in which he had abandoned realism, his own emotions too were failing him.

The disintegration of the dramatic personality is reflected in the continuing disintegration of language. In *Timon of Athens* and the Baroque comedies it verges upon incoherence; titles and pronouns are swept into the wild rush to the abyss; we get "sirs" and "shes"; the inversion of the negative—an early

[1] *The Maid's Tragedy,* II. 2.

trick of his—becomes commoner, and there are characteristic words like "pinched," "choked" (both early favorites), "ebbed," "dungy," and "earthy." So many lines end in words like "and," "but," 'if," and "that" that the verse seems to jolt—

> *O, if thou couch*
> *But one night with her, every hour in't will*
> *Take hostage of thee for a hundred, and*
> *Thou shalt remember nothing more than what*
> *That banquet bids thee to.*[2]

It is hard to believe that any audience understood more than a fraction of the dialogue which races along, well below the level of conscious thought, so that we can trace it only by its sudden rises.

The final group of plays is certainly the most difficult thing in Shakespeare to understand or explain. They are a complete reversion to a folk theater but with the folk quality left out. All have certain features in common. To begin with, they were written exclusively for an indoor theater, and with an instinctive artist like Shakespeare, not controlled, as Jonson was, by a theoretical approach to literature, apparently unimportant external details count for a lot. Exactly as Kempe's departure from the theater had encouraged the anti-realistic vein in him, so the change from the popular open-air theater with its audience of apprentices and housewives to the darkness and candlelight of the Blackfriars with its audience of courtiers is reflected in the lack of reality, either objective like

[2] *T. N. K.*, I. 1.

Falstaff's or subjective like Lear's. The change did not pass unnoticed by the writers, for though he was still popular, his reputation was on the decline as we see from Webster's malicious introduction to *The Duchess of Malfi,* where he is dismissed as a mere hack like Heywood, and Jonson's reference to "a mouldy tale like *Pericles*" and his request to the audience that "they who had graced monsters might like men."

As the creative impulse is withdrawn from the drama we see more clearly the symbolic skeleton behind. It is possible that all literature is in origin subconscious and based upon fantasias of dreams with which the conscious, intellectual mind wrestles until it has given them "a local habitation and a name"; but certainly with poets and instinctive writers, like Shakespeare, Dickens, and Ibsen, any decline in creative power at once causes the shadows of the fantasia to take over control and reduce the writer almost to a state of somnambulism. In the later comedies it is not the fantastic nature of the themes which produces the sense of unreality, but the subjective unreality which makes the themes appear so fantastic. After all, there are wilder improbabilities in *Twelfth Night* or *The Merchant of Venice* than in *Cymbeline,* but whereas the first have been passed through a realistic filter, the other has been set down with no attempt to find models in nature for Cymbeline, Posthumus, the Queen, or Imogen, so that it scarcely rises above the level of daydreaming. With a sort of dreadful neatness the characters divide themselves not so much into bad and good as into active and passive; the active, Cymbeline, Posthumus, Leontes, Polixenes, Prospero, all stamped with cruelty and hypersensibility; the passive—particularly the girls, Imogen, Perdita, and Miranda—transfigured by the blinding light of sentimentality which Shakespeare throws on them.

The pattern stands out clearly in *Cymbeline,* the least happy of the last plays. Here Cymbeline, egged on by his "fiendlike" Queen, banishes Posthumus, a young man secretly married to his daughter Imogen, whom the Queen wishes to marry to her own son, Cloten. Posthumus, as the result of a bet with a Frenchman about Imogen's faithfulness, becomes convinced of her guilt and orders his servant Pisanio to murder her. Pisanio decoys her to Milford Haven and then relents. Cloten follows her and is beheaded by outlaws (really the sons of the king, kidnapped in childhood by Belarius). Imogen, waking to find the headless body beside her, believes it is Posthumus,' and, disguised as a boy, takes service with the Roman ambassador. A Roman army comes to Britain, and the outlaws assist in defeating it, while Posthumus is captured and sentenced to death. After a recognition scene during which Cymbeline sentences practically everyone to death, all ends happily.

Except for one amusing and sardonic little scene between Cloten and Imogen, nothing in the play has been visualized, and its unreality is accentuated rather than otherwise by the stream of echoes from the great tragedies. But then occurs one scene of dreadful intensity when Posthumus is awaiting death in prison. "Hanging is the word, sir," wheezes the Gaoler. "If you be ready for that you are well cooked," and suddenly Shakespeare's interest becomes engaged. In a dreadful parody of the Duke's speech in praise of Death "which makes these odds all even" and Cleopatra's paean to that "Which shackles accidents and bolts up change, which sleeps and never palates more the dung, the beggar's nurse and Caesar's," the Gaoler cries, "But the comfort is you shall be called to no more payments; fear no more tavern bills, which are often the sadness of parting as the procuring of mirth. . . . Of this contradiction you shall now be quit. O the charity of a penny cord!" It is the Panacea once again; the icy music which blows through all the later plays with its burden of "No more, no more."

Fear no more the frown of the great
Thou art past the tyrant's stroke.

And suddenly we realize that the Gaoler with his macabre jokes is Hamlet, Macbeth, Cleopatra, and Claudio, all rolled into one. "Look you, sir, you know not which way you are going. . . . You must either be directed by some that take upon them to know, or to take upon yourself that which I am sure you do not know, or jump the after enquiry on your own peril and how you shall speed in your journey's end, I think you'll never return to tell one." [3]

I can rarely avoid a shudder at the realization that this is Shakespeare, stirred to vitality only by the symbol of the whore and hangman; that the terrible crisis of soul which had produced *Hamlet, Macbeth,* and *Antony and Cleopatra* has spent itself and descended, like the nobleman's clothes to the actor, from Hamlet to the Gaoler. It is a measure of how the storm of misanthropy has blown itself out.

The pattern repeats itself almost exactly in *A Winter's Tale*. Here Leontes, the King, suspects his

Cym., V. 4.

wife with another king, Polixenes, and after attempting to have Polixenes murdered, he orders the trial of his wife, and first the burning and then abandonment of his newborn baby, Perdita. Antigonus, the kindly old courtier who is compelled to expose her, is eaten by a bear. The Queen is cleared by the intervention of the Oracle of Apollo (about the only thing which ever could convince one of Shakespeare's jealous husbands) and is then given out for dead. Perdita, growing up as the child of a peasant in Polixenes' country, is courted by his son, Florizel, and Polixenes, who shares his fellow monarch's irascibility, neatly repeats the pattern by threatening everyone with execution. The lovers take refuge with the repentant Leontes, but are fol-lowed by Polixenes. The supposedly dead queen, made up as a statue, is then restored to her repentant hus-band, but this time the recognition scene is omitted. The title suggests indifference if not contempt, and the evasion of the recognition scene is flagrant, and em-phasized by the weary abandonment of dramatic illu-sion in passages like "There's such a deal of wonder broke out within this last hour that ballad-makers cannot be able to express it." When a dramatist writes like this he is throwing in his hand. There is a certain liveliness about the part of Autolycus, yet even this does not pass without a touch of morbidity, for he tells us how the old man's son "shall be flayed alive; then 'nointed over with honey, set on the head of a wasp's nest; then stand till he be three quarters and a dram dead; then recovered again with aqua-vitae or some other hot infusion; then raw, as he is, and in the hottest day prognostication proclaims, shall he be set against a brick wall, the sun looking with a southward eye upon him, where he is to behold him with flies blown to death."[4] We need not take the clown too seriously, but after all, Antigonus is eaten by a bear!

A Winter's Tale is as much better than *Cymbeline* as *The Tempest* than *A Winter's Tale,* for as Shakespeare abandoned the attempt at drama, he gave himself more and more to poetry, and *A Winter's Tale* is already halfway toward *The Tempest.* Drama is of a younger house.

The Tempest, one of the most beautiful poems in the world, abandons all pretense to drama; inevitably since the hero is a magician, exiled from his kingdom, who causes the shipwreck of the usurping Duke and his son; causes the son to fall in love with his own daughter, Miranda, and marries them in spite of the rather hopeless plots of Antonio and Caliban. The main difference between this and the earlier romances is that the active principle has not only absolute power in this world but in the next as well; yet even so, Prospero has still something of the hypersensibility of the tyrant and behaves in a quite ungentlemanly way with Ariel and Caliban. The great speech in which he forswears his magic is generally accepted as Shakespeare's farewell to the theater, though, as in the next twelve months he produced no less than three new plays in collaboration with John Fletcher, his farewell must be taken in the spirit of the "positively last appearance" of other eminent members of his profession.

Personally, I do not think he had any such idea in mind. That in Prospero's magic he saw something of his own is possible, but principally he saw in it a microcosm of the great magic of the universe, and

W. T., IV. 3.

in Prospero a reflection of the Creator whom, in his despairing creed, he saw as one bringing life into the world merely to destroy it. "A tale told by an idiot full of sound and fury, signifying nothing" [5] was wha it had meant to him in *Macbeth;* now it was merely "such stuff as dreams are made on." [6] The real difference is not of temper but of distance. The voice o Prospero is the voice of Macbeth, but it has disengaged itself from the coil of ambition and sin, and speaks as if from far away.

In all these later plays it is the remoteness which strikes us most forcibly. Of the three plays he wrote in collaboration with Fletcher, *Cardenio* has been lost *Henvy VIII* is mere a job of work in which Shakespeare's part is always the more vivid, but it is, as any historical play dealing with a period so close had to be mere spectacle. There was no reason on earth why *The Two Noble Kinsmen* should have been mere spectacle, but that is all it is.

There are still scholars like Tucker Brooke who refuse to admit Shakespeare's part in this play, bu that seems to me the mere negation of critical judgment. Apart from the splendor of the poetry, unequaled in any other Elizabethan writer, the style ha all the characteristics of the later Shakespeare. Ther is a bumper crop of nouns in "er": "purger," "quarter carrier," "approacher," "charmer" (not a girl but magician), "offerer," "abandoner," "confessor," "defier," "rejoicer," "decider," "corrector," and one triumphant synonym for the Creator, "Limiter"; there ar abstracts in the plural like "shames" and "decays" verbs formed of nouns like "chapel" (to take t

[5] *Macb.*, V. 5.
[6] *Tem.*, IV. 1.

church), "skiff," "bride" (marry), "ear," "jaw," and "mope" used passively, "I am moped." As usual there is the inversion of the negative as in "If he not answered."

But the play is undoubtedly a failure. The theme of the two friends in love with the same girl is one which the Shakespeare of fifteen years before would have handled with passion and certainty, but in this play he is not even interested in it. Apart from the masque scene in which the two friends and Emilia invoke Mars, Venus, and Diana (which appealed to him merely because it provided a magnificent opportunity for pure poetry) the only situation in the play which roused him to creative passion was the Antigone theme of the three queens to whom Creon refuses permission to bury their husbands. He had lost interest in lovers but was fascinated by the picture of the corpses, "showing the sun their teeth, grinning at the moon," and he who had shuddered at Yorick's skull and was to leave a curse on anyone who touched his own bones could write passionately of the three widows pleading with Hippolyta and Theseus on their wedding day (sex and death in equal balance).

He will not suffer us to burn their bones,
To urn their ashes, nor to take the offence
Of mortal loathsomeness from the blest eye
Of holy Phoebus, but infects the winds
With stench of our slain lords.[7]

But the one mistake we must avoid when considering these last plays is that of imagining that they

[7] *T. N. K.*, I. 1.

express "optimism" as Sir Edmund Chambers (who frankly dislikes them) calls it, or "reconciliation" as the editors of the New Cambridge Shakespeare are so fond of describing it. The story of the man who, having emerged from the dark pit of *Lear*, turned his eyes toward the sunlit peace of *The Tempest* (see any critical work on Shakespeare) is a pretty tale invented originally to explain to nonmusical people the difference between the Rasumowsky Quartets and the last quartets of Beethoven, and whether or not it explains that, has nothing whatever to do with Shakespeare.

On the contrary, the late comedies carry on the gloomy imagery of *Lear* and *Macbeth* and to it they add a still gloomier imagery of their own. Though for Belarius, "reverence, that angel of the world" still makes distinctions, it has almost ceased to exist elsewhere; "the odds is gone," "all mannerly distinguishment left out," and the end of the world is just round the next corner. The terrible image of the broken seed pod and the destruction of fertility which we find in *Lear, Macbeth,* and *Timon* is repeated in *A Winter's Tale* with its "Let Nature crush the sides of the world together and mar the seeds."[8] Shakespeare is still haunted by the thought of

Those that with cords, knives, drams, precipitance,
Weary of this world's light have to themselves
Been death's most horrid agents. . . .[9]

Hamlet's meditation on suicide—personal poetry if ever there was such—the cry of "That the Everlasting

[8] *W. T.*, IV. 3.
[9] *T. N. K.*, I. 1.

had not fixed his canon against self-slaughter!" [10] echoed by Cleopatra with her "Is it sin to rush into the secret house of death!" [11] is repeated in Imogen's "Against self-slaughter there is a prohibition so divine that cravens my weak hand" [12] and Posthumus' "My conscience, thou art fettered more than my shanks and wrists." [13] It is the temptation of the abyss; the "darkness my bride" theme of *Lear, Measure for Measure,* and *Antony and Cleopatra.* The "flies to wanton boys" of Lear is repeated in the invocation to Jove in *Cymbeline*—that written according to Dowden by an actor (the breed unfortunately is extinct).

No more, thou Thunder-master, show
Thy spite on mortal flies.[14]

In all of them there is, apart from the poetry, an appalling note of weariness, of which the most characteristic word is probably "ebbed," as though Shakespeare felt that the high tide of life had receded from him and left only mud behind. It occurs frequently, and with it words like "ooze" and "mud," "bottom," and "dungy" and not always in *The Tempest* where the vicinity of the sea lends it a fictitious relevance.

And the ebbed man, ne'er loved till nothing worth
Comes deared by being lacked.[15]

[10] *Ham.*, I. 2.
[11] *A. and C.*, IV. 15.
[12] *Cym.*, III. 4.
[13] *Cym.*, V. 4.
[14] *Cym.*, V. 4.
[15] *A. and C.*, I. 4.

Ebbing men indeed
Most often do so near the bottom run. . . .[16]

O melancholy,
Whoever yet could sound thy bottom? find
The ooze to show what coast thy sluggish crare
Might easiest harbour in?[17]

Therefore my son i' th' ooze is bedded and
I'll seek him deeper than e'er plummet sounded
And with him there lie mudded.[18]

I wish
Myself were mudded in that oozy bed.[19]

With Prospero's casting of his book "deeper than did ever plummet sound" they make me think less of the brisk voice of the converted pessimist than of the thud of rain in a gloomy landscape after the storm has gone by. "I like to think how Shakespear pruned his rose and ate his pippin in his orchard close" sings the greatest of Shakespearean scholars, but whenever I think of him in those last years at Stratford it is as a man like the Sibyl whom Rilke compared to an old castle "high and hollow and burnt-out." Emotionally he was dead years before they took him from New Place to Holy Trinity; a wraith of a man with inward looking eyes.

What those plays may be said to represent is stoicism; the stoicism of the old fighter with his back

[16] *Tem.*, II. 1.
[17] *Cym.*, IV. 2.
[18] *Tem.*, II. 3.
[19] *Tem.*, V. 1.

to the wall. It is as though the last drop of Christian feeling, of faith in a hereafter, and in the ultimate justification of truth and mercy had been squeezed out and replaced by that shadow of classical philosophy he had found in Montaigne with its good-humored Latin shrug of the shoulders which Shakespeare, the island-man, half Celt, half Teuton, could never emulate. It is probably no accident that from *Othello* onward he showed a preference for pagan and prehistoric themes which permitted him either to fling his scepter at the injurious gods or stoic-fashion to endure their wantonness. It was scarcely merely because the Blackfriars permitted such spectacular effects that he wrote:

Laud we the gods,
And let the crooked smoke climb to their nostrils
From our blest altars.[20]

And:

Let the temples
Burn bright with sacred fires, and the altars
In hallowed clouds commend their swelling incense
To those above us.[21]

It may be merely a fancy of mine, but I do feel there is some change in the two plays he wrote in collaboration with Fletcher, though it may be only another step in that growing remoteness from life which in *The Two Noble Kinsmen* made him choose for his first act the largely irrelevant theme of the unburied bodies. This play seems to reveal almost a fellow feeling with the

[20] *Cym.*, V. 5.
[21] *T. N. K.*, V. 1.

gods. They are no longer the wanton boys who kill us for their sport, but respectable huntsmen for whose pleasures any true follower of the chase like Shakespeare must show respect. There is something of the old humor in the way he addresses Venus, linking her with memories of his own larks in the Warwickshire deer parks.

O thou that from eleven to ninety reignest
In mortal bosoms, whose chase is this (?great) world
And we in herds thy game.[22]

And again:

The impartial gods who from their mounted heavens
View us their mortal herd.[23]

In the character of Palamon with all his innocence and idealism it is as though the ghost of his own youth were rising before him, a Troilus still undisillusioned by Cressida's lightness. Curiously, it seems to be of Troilus that he was thinking, because Troilus' cry of agony when he realizes the unfaithfulness of Cressida—"Think, we had mothers!" is Palamon's fiery reply to rakes and cynics.

I have been harsh
To large confessors, and have hotly asked them
If they had mothers? I had one, a woman,
And women 'twere they wronged.[24]

[22] *T. N. K.*, V. 1.
[23] *T. N. K.*, I. 4.
[24] *T. N. K.*, V. 1.

The bitterness against women too has gone, and the wonderful poetry, clear, calculated, and full of muscle, is the nearest he ever reached to true classical quality, as in that unforgettable epitaph on a girl:

Who made too proud the bed took leave of the moon.[25]

Or the First Queen's wild balancing of the marriage night with the corpses on the field of Thebes.

When her arms
Able to lock Jove from a synod, shall
By warranting moonlight corslet thee, O when
Her twinning cherries shall their sweetness fall
Upon thy tasteful lips, what wilt thou think
Of rotton kings or blubbered queens? what care
For what thou feel'st not, what thou feel'st being able
To make Mars spurn his drum? [26]

As I say, it may be only fancy, but for me it is as though once more the rock of personality had split; the old huntsman has become the stag at bay, remembering his own youth and all the joys of the chase, and forgives the gods even as they strike him. Once more the ghost of Tarquin is with him, and the theme of the faithless friend is mingled with that of the impartial gods, but by now Shakespeare's spirit is so remote that even ingratitude and unfaithfulness are no more than the sport of children playing under his window in the light that fades over the Malvern Hills. The voice we hear is Shakespeare's but it seems to come from an immense distance, until it too fades forever.

[25] *T. N. K.*, I. 3.
[26] *T. N. K.*, I. 1.

O you heavenly charmers,
What things you make of us! For what we lack
We laugh; for what we have are sorry, still
Are children in some kind. Let us be thankful
For that which is. . . .[27]

About the Author

FRANK O'CONNOR (pseudonym of Michael O'Donovan) was born in Cork, Ireland, in 1903. Though he says that he received no education worth mentioning and has had no ambitions except to write, he is nevertheless widely respected for his professional abilities as a librarian, for his knowledge of architecture and music as well as of numerous languages, and for his accomplishments as a dramatist.

Mr. O'Connor's first published book was *Guests of the Nation,* a volume of short stories. He later published novels, several additional volumes of tales, *The Mirror in the Roadway* (a study of the modern novel), verse, travel books, and a study of Michael Collins and the Irish Revolution. He has lived in the United States since 1952 and taught at Harvard as well as at Northwestern University. Readers of *The New Yorker, Holiday,* and *Esquire* are familiar with Mr. O'Connor's stories and sketches.

[27] *T. N. K.,* V. 4.